Edmund Noble

The Russian Revolt

Its Causes, Condition and Prospects

Edmund Noble

The Russian Revolt
Its Causes, Condition and Prospects

ISBN/EAN: 9783337168162

Printed in Europe, USA, Canada, Australia, Japan

Cover: Foto ©ninafisch / pixelio.de

More available books at **www.hansebooks.com**

THE

RUSSIAN REVOLT

ITS

CAUSES, CONDITION, AND PROSPECTS

BY

EDMUND NOBLE

BOSTON
HOUGHTON, MIFFLIN AND COMPANY
New York: 11 East Seventeenth Street
The Riverside Press, Cambridge
1885

CONTENTS.

	PAGE
NOMADIC SURVIVALS	5
APOLISM	35
ENVIRONMENT	57
OLD RUSSIAN LIFE	76
BYZANTINISM AND THE THREE UNITIES	93
DOMESTIC SLAVERY	110
THE RELIGIOUS PROTEST	126
WESTERN ENLIGHTENMENT	145
FIRST FRUITS	160
MYSTICISM AND PESSIMISM	179
THE DYNAMIC PERIOD	193
PERSONAL CHARACTERISTICS	212
MODERN IRRITATIONS	231
EUROPE AND THE REVOLT: THE FUTURE	252

THE RUSSIAN REVOLT.

NOMADIC SURVIVALS.

THE Russian plain, as I saw it almost unintermittingly during a ten days' journey in the summer of 1882, has a strange power of reproducing some of those illusions that are properly called marine. At sea most people have noticed how largely the apparent extent of the prospect offered to the eye of a spectator depends on the state of the waters, or rather upon the particular character of their surface at the moment of observation. Should the waves run high, presenting their optical effect in a comparatively few concentrated masses of large dimensions, the sense of extension is weakened, and the sky line made to assume a nearness not its due. But when the disturbance is over, and there are left only tiny waves, little more than ripples, the horizon seems to have receded to a distance relatively immense. It is this false vastness of surface, suggested to the eye by

great multiplicity and regularity, as well as
minuteness, of detail, that gives so much of its
aspect to the landscape of European Russia,
and to a traveler, plodding day after day over
steppe and plain, seems to swell a territory by
no means in need of exaggeration into dimensions almost too abnormal for even the imagination.   And the sensation is the same whether
one experience it in the barren governments of
the southeast, or amid the activities of communal agriculturists in the rich regions of the
" black earth."   Summer or winter, seed time
or harvest, the same smooth plateau widens out
as the eye follows to its union with the sky,
and the same circular rim bounds vision with a
line that often looks regular enough to be made
the base of an astronomical calculation.   Un-
dulations of surface are very rare, and when
met with sometimes denote mere fluent masses
of sand or mud-dust that hàve been capriciously
arranged by the wind.   Interruptions of the
monotony are, in fact, so insignificant that,
instead of serving as correctives, they actually
seem to add to the general sense of flatness,
whether it be conveyed by plain, forest, or
town.

At a very early period of its history, Russia
in Europe was all but overrun by forests.   To-
day the traveler may cross vast tracts of the

country without seeing a single tree. According to some native writers, nothing more is needed than the destruction of a few woods to turn the whole of European Russia into a "desert steppe." [1] The absence of accessible stone formations, and particularly of mountains, is more marked still. Hence, no doubt, the attraction which all hill scenery has to the modern Russian. It is a strange fact, moreover, that to mountain scapes, Russian literature is indebted for some of its finest productions. Exiled, as each of them was at different times, to the Caucasus Mountains, both Pushkin and Lermontov [2] found rich stores of poetic material in that sublime range. All who know this part of the country will agree with me when I say that scarcely any contrast in scenery can be conceived at all so striking or so likely to preside at the birth of new ideas as the contrast thus offered between the flat land of European Russia and the heights of which Pushkin wrote : —

"Eternal thrones of snow,
Whose lifted summits gloom to the gaze
Like one unbroken, motionless chain of clouds;
And in their midst the twin-peaked colossus,

---

[1] "Pustinnaya step." St. Petersburg *Novosti*, Oct. 4, 1883.

[2] Griboyedov, another Russian author, wrote also within sight of the Caucasus his celebrated comedy, *The Misfortune of Having Brains.*

> The giant monarch of mountains, Elbrus,
> Whitens up into heaven's blue deep."

That mountains are not commonplace objects in Russia, and that the Eastern Slav must travel for them to the Ural chain, to the Caucasus, or to Switzerland, seems even to have attained a certain expression in the proverbial philosophy of the common people, who speak of things at a great distance as "beyond the mountains."[1]

To what extent, then, and in what especial manner, has the course of history and civilization in Russia been influenced by physical peculiarities of contour and surface? What does the Great Russian owe to race, and what to geographical position? Underlying all possible answers that may be given to these questions are two facts on which some emphasis should be laid; for not only have the Russians been exposed to a series of peculiar influences not paralleled by any single case of racial development in western Europe, but all Russian phenomena of to-day, be they social, political, religious, or literary, will be found to have a special character, rendering their reconciliation with apparently inter-related phenomena in other countries wholly impossible. M. Pelle-

---

[1] "Za gorami." This is scarcely related to the German "über alle Berge."

tan [1] says happily that every civilization has an
involuntary *collaborateur* within its own territory; and in Russia the influence of this silent
helper must have been immense. The " country of plains," as the historian Soloviev calls it,
was from the first marked out for a kind of
development fundamentally different from that
of the older western civilizations. Plains invite to movement and migration, just as hills
and mountains attach men to particular spots
of the earth's surface. In European Russia
this wandering tendency had special circumstances in its favor, since, while it was often
nothing more than a protest against absolutism
and centralization, it actually formed one of the
indispensable conditions of the national development.

Nor could migratory movements fail to be
largely promoted by influences such as those of
race, intermingling, and environment. Let us
suppose for a moment that the Great Russian
started his racial career as a genuine Slav of the
purest Aryan stock. It by no means necessarily
follows that his lineal descendant of to-day has
no Turanian blood in his veins, no Asiatic customs in the various forms of his social and religious life. The theory of a pure Slav race of
Great Russians has ceased to have attraction

[1] *Profession de Foi du XIX Siècle.* Paris.

even for the Slavs themselves. It is not in accordance with well-known facts. In the earlier part of their national existence, the Russians occupied scarcely a fifth part of the territory which they claim in the Europe of to-day. On the north and east and southeast they were closely hemmed in by races of Turanian origin, of wandering habits and Asiatic customs. They lived in every-day contact with the Finns, the Cheremiss, the Pechenegs, the Mordvs, and Kazars. What, then, became of these peoples in the gradual expansion of the Slav colonies to the north and west? Were they simply driven back into Asia?

The evidence available shows that these Tatar-Turkish races were in a large measure absorbed. The Finnish traits of many Russian faces seen in the northern cities clearly testify to blood alliances on the part of the Slavs with their nomad neighbors, while in the west, according to Mr. Wallace, race-intermingling has left its mark upon whole districts. Transmission of habits, moreover, must have taken place quite independently of alliances such as these. M. Soloviev, in explaining the difference between Russian and west European customs, expressly alludes, not only to internal causes, but to "the constant contact and relations of the Russians with Asiatic peoples, providing for the absorption of the latter and for the transmission of their habits."[1]

What, again, is absorption? Not a few writers use the term as if it were synonymous with disappearance. This is a manifest error. A type can no more cease to be than the materials of which it is composed. The function of much of this so-called "dying out" seems to be the very useful one of preparing a new race for new conditions by a process of acclimatization much more rapid than the ordinary one of air and food. In some cases absorption serves as a sort of drawbridge over which inferior peoples hasten from adverse conditions to a place of racial safety. If, therefore, where absorption took place, the early Slavs contributed to the new ethnological modification such elements as character, energy, daring, initiative, intellect, enterprise, the nomads giving form, structure, some habits and more traditions, we can easily understand how a glow of new life would arise in the men of the plains, and how to the Slavs would come, it may be, hereditary memories of a more eastern existence, hereditary sympathies with wild movements and migrations, of which the only sentiment of nationality was the sense of numbers, the likeness of faces, the community of purpose. But a speculation such as this in-

[1] *Uchebnaya Kniga russkoy Istorii.*

dicates only the kind of influence likely to be
exerted upon the Slav colonies by the Tataric
populations of Eastern Russia. Leaving aside
all supposition or inference, the fact remains,
of an absolute certainty, that the processes mentioned — of race-intermingling on the one hand,
and close ethnological contact on the other —
were continued through very considerable periods of time, and that each tended to the
modification of the Russian character by the
transference of racial habits and customs.

The Mongol invasion still further helped to
give an Asiatic turn to the earlier forms of Russian civilization. Remembering that for two
hundred years the country was occupied and
dominated by men of high cheek-bones, of eyes
set obliquely, and of sallow visage, speaking a
Tatar tongue, one cannot think it strange that
Asiatic traits should now and then rise to the
ethnological surface of modern Russia. Some
historians attach little, others great, importance
to the Tatar period of Russian history. National sensitiveness and pride have influenced
native writers on this subject when they have
thought themselves most impartial, yet M. Gri-
goriev, a St. Petersburg professor, writes: —

"There was a time when Orthodox Russia seemed
thoroughly Tatar. Everything in it except its religion was permeated and impregnated with Tatardom,

in the same degree, if not more so, as it is now impregnated with Western ideas. . . . Not only in externals — in dress, manners, and habits of life — did the Russian princes and boyards, the Russian officials and merchants, imitate the Tatars, but in everything — their feelings, ideas, and aspirations in the region of practical life — they were in the strongest way influenced by Tatardom. Our ancestors received this Tatar influence during two hundred years, at first from an unwilling, but afterwards from an habitual conformity to the tone and manners and morals that reigned at Sarai,[1] which in those times bore the same relation to us as subsequently fell to the lot of Paris. . . . During the whole of the Moscow period up to the time of Peter the Great, the statecraft and political management of the Russian Tsars and magnates continued to be in every respect Tatar. So that without acquaintance with real Tatardom it is impossible correctly to understand many phases in Russian history."

The more superficial results of the Mongol domination are easily discovered. The traveler cannot bargain with the droshky driver in St. Petersburg without hearing words that were imported into Russian from an Asiatic speech. The Russian habit of eating food, usually rice, in commemoration of dead relatives, is clearly of Tatar origin. When Russian funeral processions pause for a few mo-

---

[1] Seat of the Mongol Khans.

ments at churches in their line of march, they
are doing precisely what certain Turanian races
do on like occasions in Central Asia.   To call
the residence of royalty at St. Petersburg the
" Above," or " Tip-Top " (*Verkh*), is a habit of
speech borrowed from a purely nomad fashion
of designating the official domiciles of semi-bar-
barian monarchs beyond the Urals.   For a
considerable period of the national history, opu-
lent Russians wore the *tafya*, or skull-cap, now
in use among the Sarts of Tashkent, and the
Tatar Mahommedans ; like the men of the desert, they shaved their heads.[1]   Many Russian
dances are of Asiatic origin.   The Russian
equivalents for " dog," " water-melon," " night-
cap," " shoe," " boot," " belt," " cossack," are
all borrowed from Tatar languages.   *Kvas*, the
popular Russian drink, is generally used in
China.   *Med*, also a Russian beverage, was
known to the barbarous races of Central Asia.

The striking similarity between the Tatar
customs of to-day and the Russian customs of
three centuries ago is shown by the following
juxtaposed extracts descriptive of the two
periods : —

[1] *Ocherk domashnei zhizni i nravov velikorusskavo naroda v
xvi i xvii stolyetiakh.* N. I. Kostomarava. Page 103.

Moscow. — First Half of 16th Century.

The prince himself pointed to the seat, both by word and gesture. When we had duly saluted the prince from this spot, the interpreter translated our communication. After hearing our salutation, he arose, and descending from his seat, said, " Is our brother Charles, Emperor and Supreme King of the Romans, well ? " To which the Count replied, " He is well." Ascending the steps, he called each of us to him and said, " Give me thy hand ; hast thou traveled well on thy journey? " To which each of us replied, " Heaven grant that thou mayst live in health many years. By the grace of God and thy favor, I have been well."... It is the custom, after dinner, for him to say to the ambassadors, " Now you may depart." — *Interview with Vassily Ivanovich.* HERBERSTEIN.

Central Asia. — 1874.

As I drew near, the masters of the ceremonies uttered the usual loud cry, " God, make his majesty, Amir Mozaffar, powerful and victorious ! "... As I entered the tent, the Amir turned and smilingly held out his hand, took mine, and said, " General, Aman ! Is the General well ? " I replied, " Aman, he is well." He then gave his hand to the interpreter and motioned to us to sit down facing him at the end of the tent. .... I thanked him for the permission, and waited a moment longer. He began to look uneasily towards the door. The taksuba appeared, and the Amir said, " Now, go ! " upon which we immediately took our leave. — *Interview with the Bek of Khitab, Bukhara.* SCHUYLER.

Russia. — First Half of 16th Century.

They [the Russians] observe this custom in meeting ambassadors going to Russia. They send a messenger to the ambassador to desire him to alight from his horse or carriage. . . . The delegate takes watchful heed not to alight first from his horse or carriage, lest by doing so he should seem to derogate from his master's dignity, and will not alight until he has first seen the ambassador dismount. — HERBERSTEIN.

Central Asia. — 1874.

Three miles from town, I met the assistant of the Bek [of Khitab], with his suite, when we all alighted and embraced one another, each, however, taking particular pains not to derogate from his dignity by alighting too soon. I had soon learnt whether to dismount first or last, or whether to watch the motions of the dignitary who met me, and so manage it that we should put our feet on the ground at one and the same moment. — SCHUYLER.

Turgeniev wrote somewhere: "With my eyes shut, listening in Russia to the rustling of the leaves, I should be able to tell the season, or even the month of the year." The Russian novelist had a faculty not at all common to dwellers in west European cities. Indeed, the conditions of our older civilizations neither produce acuteness of the senses, nor encourage its survival. The Slavs, on the other hand, boast of the sharpness of their vision, and the whiteness of their teeth; their physical powers of endurance could scarcely be greater had they directly descended from the followers of Chingis Khan. On this point both Kinglake and Vereshchagin pay the most willing testimony. On the intellectual side of the question, the evidence is rather scant. It is a fact that the *schot*, or counting frame, is used all over Russia, in the simplest as well as the most complicated arithmetical operations, by the lowest as well as the highest in the land. In Russia nobody seems capable of performing the simplest sum in addition or subtraction without help from the counting frame. I have seen a merchant deliberately take down the wires and balls in order, by putting two rows of the latter side by side, to ascertain that five and five made ten. Government officials perform the most trifling calculations in the same way.

This perpetual use of the *schot* may seem to justify the inference that Russian mental powers are at fault. No more erroneous assumption could be even imagined. In the faculty of remembering, in receptivity for knowledge of all kinds, the Great Russian carries off the palm from all western competitors. Hence his proficiency in acquiring languages. In this single capacity lies reflected the whole busy world of racial movement within which Slav development took place. The Russian may inherit much of his receptivity from con-

2

stantly repeated processes of adaptation to new circumstances and varying conditions; but his memory is a racial characteristic and belongs to the blood. It has been suggested that Russians are easily linguists, because of special training in languages and of unusual facilities for acquiring them. The fact that most Russian families of the wealthier class are brought up in constant intercourse with foreign governesses and tutors proves nothing. Imported foreign governesses and tutors do not prevent many English families from acquiring their proficiency in foreign speech abroad. It must be remembered that in Russia this linguistic faculty is diffused in a very democratic fashion through all classes of society, priests and peasants alone excepted. Take the case of Russian students. A large number of them are very poor. Many of these ardent lovers of knowledge would never enjoy college or university education at all, were it not for the stipends they receive from the government. In some cases, these stipends cover the cost of food and lodging, as well as of tuition. Yet it is exceedingly rare to meet with a Russian student who does not converse fluently in either French or German. Often the youth speaks both, and has a reading knowledge of other languages as well. It has been suggested that the Russians have a superior system of

teaching languages. This is the worst explanation of all, since a born linguist will acquire
languages under the worst possible system, even
without a system at all; and no nation ever
yet succeeded in maintaining a monopoly in
methods of education. I must urge, therefore,
that Russian facility in languages is a natural
and not a merely acquired art, that it is a racial
characteristic, favored in its development by
peculiar circumstances of ethnological growth,
reference to which will be made hereafter. It
is this view of the matter that accounts for the
acquirements of the father of Vladimir Monomakh, who is said to have learned five languages without quitting his palace; and this
view, also, that explains the ease and rapidity
with which in these days Russians domiciled
abroad adapt themselves to the lingual and social conditions of their new environment.

Habit and racial characteristics thus give
coincident testimony as to the conditions of
Russian development, both showing, however
faintly, that its main features were restlessness,
movement, migration. The evidence of history
is stronger still. In its light we see how to
the baby Slav, barely out of its cradle, destiny
offered immense *Völkerwanderungen* as specta-
cles. Nearly all the great historic processions
entered Europe by way of Russia; vast as was

the road, touching barbarism on the one hand,
civilization on the other, there were times when
it seemed scarcely broad enough for the march
of the races that, beginning with Hun and end-
ing with Mongol, swarmed over it in almost
uninterrupted succession. With such an environment around him, the Slav soon began migratory movements on his own account. The
openness of the land invited the exploits of the
druzhiniki under their *kniaz;* a warlike spirit
led to expeditions against the Turanian foe.
Later, recoiling from Mongol exaction, attracted
by the virgin soil of the great plains to the east,
the Russians spread in ever increasing waves,
until at last all the European territory of their
present empire lay at the feet of the Slav colonist. Nor was this process, which ultimately
carried the Russian emigrants into Siberia, one
of mere expansion alone. It went on in European Russia as a phase of the restlessness which
in those days seemed to characterize all forms
of life amongst the Slavs. There were wandering migrations as well as colonizing migrations.
The working agriculturists rambled from estate
to estate, from district to district, from government to government. The movement at last
grew to such dimensions and had so disastrous
an effect upon the national finances that, as a
preventive measure, the laborer had to be at-

tached to the glebe. Migrant habits thus led to that characteristic feature of Russian civilization, the enslavement of the tillers of the soil; and if, anticipating somewhat, we look at a much later period of Russian history, we shall find that the need of migration to serfs dying off prematurely for lack of changed conditions was one of the arguments used and acted upon in favor of the emancipation *ukaz* of 1861.[1] The movement was in great part checked by the preventive measures of Boris Godunov, yet serfs oppressed by masters did not scruple to resume their earlier habits; the Don Cossacks were for long periods recruited by fugitives of this class. Tension in religious circles also gave a powerful impulse to migration. Sectarians, intolerant of the ecclesiastical order of things imported from Constantinople and imposed upon the people with the aid of Mongol blood, fled across the country, and plunging through trackless woods, wandering by the shores of lakes and seas, sought out quiet refuges for their ideals in religion. One of the protesting sects bears to this day the name " Stranníki," or Wanderers, its leading dogma being the necessity of "a perpetual wandering from Antichrist." Another body of dissenters, calling themselves " Christ seekers," wander from town

---

[1] See Turgeniev's *Zapiski Okhotniki.*

to town, and from one government to another, in the hope of meeting the Saviour.[1]

Most of the historical migrations have ceased with the immediate causes which called them into being; but the habit of wandering, of movement from place to place, has not disappeared from Russia. New forms have been given to it by railways and steamboats. Siberia swarms with escaped convicts, whose wanderings and depredations have brought into existence the sport known as "vagabond hunting." [2] The conditions created by emancipation favored the development of a class of laborers, half peasants, half artisans, who are confirmed migrants, spending part of the year in the country, the remainder of it in the town. In a sense, even religion is migrant in Russia. The *lavra* of Sergius is said to attract over a million pilgrims every year.[3] Kiev, with its tombs, icons, and relics, is also a spot where thousands of the orthodox annually gather from all parts of the Russian empire. Numerous fairs encourage movement at stated times in the year. Workmen rarely remain for any considerable period in one factory or district. The vastness of the

[1] *Raskolniki i Ostrozhniki.* By Fiodor Vassilievich Livanov. St. Petersburg, 1873.

[2] "Okhota na brodyag." See an article in the now defunct Review, *Otechestvenny Zapiski.* Nov., 1882.

[3] St. Petersburg *Golos,* 1865. No. 283.

country, moreover, gives a migratory character
to almost all forms of the movement of travel.
Students who journey to St. Petersburg from
the southern, central, or eastern governments of
Russia, in order to spend several years of an
educational course in a city which must become
their home for that period, are as truly migrants
as the early Russian colonists who settled territories east of the Urals, or as the Tatars who
travel from Central Asia in order to wait at
table in the hotels of St. Petersburg. And it
may be more than a political instinct that leads
so many Russians to exchange habitat with
these swarthy sons of the desert. What especially surprises a foreigner unaccustomed in
Western Europe to eastern aspects of migration
is the very large number of Russians domiciled
on the banks of the Neva, whose homes may be
at a distance of thousands of versts; equally
striking is the apparent ease with which even
the poorest peasants make their way from one
end of this vast empire to the other. The effect of great extent of territory in enlarging
one's ideas of travel is a common experience;
the Russian never seems more at home than
when *en voyage*. Whether in the telega, the
railway carriage, or the steamboat, he rarely be-
trays consciousness either of distance or of di-
vorce from any particular part of the territory

which he calls his fatherland. The lines of railway seem at times to encourage wide views of this kind, since some of them, in their effort to compass vast distances, ignore large cities lying almost directly in their path. Thus the Russian locomotive is made to pass within two miles or less of such important centres of population as Tver, Orol, and Kursk. It is noteworthy that the word for "play" in Russian literally means "to walk." A child told that when a lesson is over it shall "go to walk" (*idi gulyat*) anticipates play, not promenade. A wife unfaithful to her husband is said to "walk away" from him (*gulyaet ot muzha*).

The evidence of language ought not to be lightly passed over. It will be found, as a rule, that wherever the racial habits and physical peculiarities of a people tend to create settled forms of social life; to discourage movement and lead to the aggregation of masses in particular districts and centres; to cause attachment to particular parts of a country apart from attachment to it as a whole, — there dialects will inevitably come into existence. The circumstances are somewhat analogous to those under which pools and lagoons, originally deposited by a main stream, but finally severed from it, suffer from the cutting of their connection with the fresh waters. In countries where there is no migration to preserve the homogeneousness of the spoken tongue, districts become isolated from districts, towns from towns, people from people. There being no general diffusion of the standard customs of speech, differentiations take place, and from small departures the change goes on, until the people of one district or county become with difficulty intelligible to those of another. Such a process has taken place in almost all the older countries of Europe, notably in Greece, Italy, Germany, and France. The case of England is also of good illustrative value. The Saxon heptarchy in that country was once a heptarchy of dialects. Even to-day it needs a special study to qualify for reading in the Yorkshire, Lancashire, and Somersetshire varieties of the spoken tongue. A cockney brought up within the sound of Bow Bells would be lingually far more at home in New York than in the cottage of many a Rochdale cotton operative. Let us now turn to European Russia. Here is a country larger than all the rest of Europe put together, yet utterly devoid of dialects.[1] From the Baltic to the Caspian, from the Krim to the North Sea, wherever Great Russian is spoken by Great Russians, its pro-

[1] Polish, developed under different conditions, has a number of dialects, but is a member of the Slavic family — an independent speech, and not a dialect of Great Russian. Nor is Little Russian a dialect in the usual acceptation of the term.

nunciation is practically the same.[1] And it is
this capacity for being intelligible over a very
wide area that is one of the characteristic features of Turanian (Asiatic) languages.   An
Osmanli from Constantinople can, it is said,
make himself understood by a Yakut on the
Lena.   Ethnologists, while not accepting this
statement without qualification, admit that the
Turkish languages, when separated by enormous distances, are strangely alike.[2]

Nor is this all.   In its very texture and composition, the Russian language bears witness to
the conditions under which Slav development
took place.   Max Müller writes: —

" It is an indispensable requirement in a nomad language that it should be intelligible to many, though
their intercourse be but scanty.   It requires traditions, society, and literature to maintain forms which
can no longer be analyzed at once. . . . In the ever-
shifting state of a nomadic society, no debased coin
can be tolerated in language, no obscure legend accepted on trust.   The metal must be pure and the
legend distinct, that the one may be weighed and the
other, if not deciphered, at least recognized as a well-
known guarantee.   Hence the small proportion of
irregular forms in all agglutinative languages."

Now, Russian is not a nomad tongue, but a

---

[1] The enunciation of the *o* is not always uniform.
[2] *Völkerkunde*, by Oscar Peschel.

member of the Indo-European family of languages, yet some of its peculiarities approximate
in a striking manner to those described as requisite to the speech of a wandering people. The
agglutinative power of the language is noticed
by Professor Sayce,[1] who further observes: "In
Russian the participles have replaced the aorist
and imperfect, which have also been lost in
Ruthenian, though retained in Servian and Bul-
garian; and in this change we may perhaps
trace the influence of those Tatar tribes whose
blood enters so largely into that of the modern
Russian community." [2] But the testimony may
be carried much further than the extent to
which Professor Sayce draws upon it. Take
the case of irregular forms, of which we have
seen nomad languages to be so intolerant. The
tongues of settled races are overrun with them.
French has 72 irregular verbs, Romaic 88,
Swedish 141, German 217, Italian 514. The
number of irregular verbs in Russian is 13. It
is requisite to the language of a migratory people that its forms shall be intelligible at a
glance — that as little shall be left to the context as possible. Russian leaves nothing to the
context. "Love" in English may be either a

---

[1] *Introduction to the Science of Language*, vol. ii., p. 95.
[2] I quote Professor Sayce's statement for philological rather than
for historic purposes.

verb or a noun. The noun in Russian is "lyu-
bov;" the verb "lyubit." Russian verbs, moreover, go armed with a whole paraphernalia of
variations, insuring a closeness of analysis, an
exactness of definition, and a general intelligibility that in most modern Indo-European
tongues would appear altogether superfluous.
For a learner to use accurately a Russian verb,
he must first decide whether he wishes to express completed action, incompleted action,
single action, plurality of action, single perfect action, or commencing action. Supposing
"spoke," the past tense of speak, were Russian,
the choice would lie between such forms as
"*na*spoke" ("I spoke" — completed action),..
"sp*u*ke" ("I spoke once" — semelfactive),
"spa*vo*ke" ("I spoke more than once" — iter-
ative), "*za*spoke" ("I began to speak" —
commencing action), and "spoke" ("I was
speaking" — incompleted action). This striv-
ing after precision and intelligibility is further
seen in nouns expressing relationship. Instead
of using forms possessing a certain inter-resem-
blance, such as "father-in-law," "mother-in-
law," "*beau-père*," "*beau-frère*," etc., the Russian language has separate terms for presenting
the distinctions between the father of the wife
and the father of the husband, the mother of
the wife and the mother of the husband, and so

on, throughout the inter-relationships of blood and marriage. Russian patronymics illustrate the same habits of language. Greater closeness of description is obtained in names by adding the paternal designation, so that, instead of a man being called Peter Orlov, or a woman Mary Romanov, he becomes " John Orlov's Peter," and she " Vassily Romanov's Mary." [1] I shall only add that in Russian there are few homonyms, and an almost complete absence of phonetic resemblances like " wright," " right," " rite," " write," etc.

The eating habits of modern Russians are not altogether without traces of the influence of primitive custom and race environment. It is well known that life on the plains — whether it be spent in hunting or have a pastoral character — leads to irregularity in eating. Such an existence tends, owing to the long fasts often involved, to encourage the merging of several small meals into a single substantial one, capable of carrying the hunter or agriculturist over the needs of, say, a whole day. Herberstein,[2] writing in the sixteenth century, speaks of Russians who, having had one good dinner, abstained from meat for two or three days. Meals at

[1] Literally, "The Johnian Peter Orlov," "the Vassilyan Mary Romanov."

[2] German ambassador to the court of Ivan Vassilievich at Moscow.

stated hours, at the rate of three and four in the day, could only be taken when a regular division had been made in the hours of daily labor, and this division implies a well-developed urban organization. In Russia a tendency lingers to postpone eating until the middle of the day, — that is to say, until the midday meal. Breakfast is almost ignored by large classes of the population. It rarely consists of more than a glass of weak tea, with a small morsel of bread or cake added on rare occasions. Yet on the strength of such light pabulum as this I have seen active officials and business men sally forth for five hours of the most arduous work of the day. For tea, which is a meal scarcely more substantial than breakfast, there is no distinctive name in Russian, the invitation to it being simply, "Come to drink tea!"[1]

The noticeable characteristic of Russian food is the ease with which it is prepared, and the facility with which it may be carried about. The consumption of dried fish is exceedingly large; very small kinds of fish are eaten raw. The joke about candle-eating in Russia probably arose out of the fact that in the territory of the river Kura the minoga (*petromyson fluviatilis*), a sort of fluvial lamprey, is dried for use as a candle or torch. The native cookery, on the other

---

[1] "Idítyĕ chai pit."

hand, is of the simplest. The people, for the most part, eat bread without butter. In "table manners" the Russians are fond of excelling. Yet, under special circumstances, two persons, falling to with fork, may eat out of a single plate without committing any breach of social propriety. This survival has a smack of atavism about it, since in the sixteenth and seventeenth century, as mentioned by Mr. Kostomarov,[1] it was the custom to seat guests at table at the rate of two to a plate. The Russian habit of sleeping after meals has a still higher historical justification. That severe code of domestic morals, the "Domostroï,"[2] expressly warns the guest not to remain too long, in order that the host's postprandial siesta may not be interfered with. Why this fashion of midday slumber survived in Russia will be best set forth in the succeeding chapter: that it would speedily disappear amid the feverish urban and industrial activities of Western Europe is evident.

Two habits remain, which there is the strongest ground for describing as primarily due to the influences of steppe life upon the physical organism. The Russians have a marked aversion to water, and a liking not less strong for tea. The same choice of tea as beverage, with

---

[1] "*Ocherk*," etc.   [2] From the fifteenth century.

the same dislike of water as its exciting cause,
is found amongst the races of the desert and
plain in Asia, notably the Tatars, Kalmucks,
and Khirgiz. In categorical, if somewhat unfortunate connection with the predilection for tea
stands the habit of spitting; whatever this may
mean in other countries, when Russians expec-
torate it is a sign of disgust. In his romance,
" Smoke," Turgeniev mentions the publication
at Heidelberg by a group of Russian emigrants
of a journal, on the title-page of which appeared the words, " À tout venant je crache."
The habit is frequently pointed to in Slav literature. As I write Zacharjasiewicz's Polish
novel " Na Kresach " is lying before me. On
the first page of the first chapter occur these
words : " Maciejaszek splunal trzy razy i prze-
zegnal sie," — " Maciejaszek spat three times
and crossed himself." The " Domostroï " enjoins its readers not to spit carelessly at table,
but rather to spit with caution, and then to
destroy the evidences of the act with the foot.
A habit that could meet with such realistic justification as this from the pen of an ecclesiastical
dignitary and state counselor must have had a
more solid ethnological foundation than that of
mere coarseness of manners. Are we not justified in seeking its origin in some wide steppe or
desert land, where the flying sand-dust was with

difficulty prevented from entering eyes, ears, nostrils, and mouth, and where an act of expectoration became an act of cleanliness not unnaturally associated with a temporary feeling of disgust?

On the whole, the justification seems abundant and irresistible that, partly because of racial and inherited tendencies, partly owing to influence of environment and race-intermingling, as well as to contagiousness of habits, manners, and customs, and partly, as the more secular cause, in consequence of the general circumstances of a peculiar national development, the Russians are more remarkable than any other people of Aryan blood for the ease with which they change the place of their domicile, and for the migrant character of their lives and activities. It is fair, moreover, to say that these characteristics have played a highly important part in giving its form, its institutions, and its difficulties, to the modern Russian state. And while, on the one hand, migrant habits have tended to stimulate that pride of individuality, that love of liberty and of free institutions which, as I shall hereafter show, form the foundation of the Slav character and genius, on the other they have weakened the resistance of the masses and facilitated the arrangements of absolute power. Russian energies

3

have been largely dispersed in steppe and plain. Engaged in colonizing vast tracts of virgin territory rather than in improving the apparatus and increasing the comfort of life within the confines of towns, they have had few opportunities of bringing into existence any robust conception of urban independence and civic rights. This phenomenon of apolism — this meagre development of towns and town activities — came to be the natural corollary of migrant, unsettled habits. How it manifested itself, and what were its results, will be shown in the succeeding chapter.

APOLISM.

THE facts of city life in Russia, whether regarded as results or merely as concomitant phenomena, will be found quite in harmony with the conditions of national development already set forth. Circumstances inimical to the spirit of urban life have hindered the growth of Russian towns from the first. The early Slavs not only were without conception of city existence, but did not even live in houses. Karamzin[1] mentions the names of four tribes of Russian Slavs who dwelt habitually in the woods; the same historian cites testimony concerning Slavs of the Danube, who had their retreats in wild, marshy, and inaccessible places.[2] Another writer describes the Slavs as possessing neither horses, arms, nor houses, and as protecting themselves from the weather by means of interlaced branches of trees. It is tolerably certain that at a somewhat later period than that here referred to the Russians lived

[1] *Istoria gosudarstva rossiïskavo.*

[2] "Paludes sylvasque pro civitatibus habent." Jordan. M. Popul.

in a highly primitive form of *oppida*, known in the modern language as *gorodishchay ;* remains of these structures, consisting of ramparts of earth surmounted with palisading, are found to this day, usually on eminences, the high banks of rivers, or in other positions equally strategic. Of one thing we may be certain, — the first Russian houses must have had wood as the material of their construction, since stone was almost unattainable, while the supply of timber, the country having a plenitude of forests, was practically inexhaustible. It is impossible, therefore, to connect the materials of early Russian housebuilding with the habits of the builders. It may even well enough be that the enforced use of wood, leading to the perpetual conflagrations that everywhere light up the pages of Russian history, helped to intensify the unsettled character of the national life. The popular belief, transmitted to the present day, that every house in Russia is destined soon or late to be burned to the ground, was not, at any rate, calculated to strengthen affection for a particular domicile.

Etymologically, the Russian city, or *gorod*, is still an "inclosure," or place inclosed, corresponding with the West-European *bourg*. For town the Russians write *posad*, the equivalent of *stadt* (*stätte*) in German and *miasto* in

Polish; that is to say, "place;" while the
Russian village is simply *derevnya*, or "the
wooden." But the characteristic features of
the Russian *gorod* only appear when we ex-
amine the city in its relation to the country at
large. Compared with urban growth in western Europe, town life in Russia is strikingly
insignificant. Scarcely a tenth part of the population of European Russia is urban; in England nearly half the people live in the towns
and cities. Nor is the tenth part named any
fixed quantity. It merely represents the time
when urban Russia is fullest, owing to the
periodical influx of a part of the population
which is, strictly speaking, neither urban nor
rural, but belongs to both country and town.

Gogol must have remarked this insignificance
of the urban element; for in his novel, "Dead
Souls," the humorist compares Russian cities to
"tiny dots that indistinctly mark the centre of
some vast plain."[1] That the peculiarity is not
confined to one branch of the Slav family may
be gathered from an expression, singularly
identical with that of Gogol, by which Hüppe[2]
compares the cities of the old Polish Slavs to
"drops of oil on a pond." Urban phenomena

---

[1] See Gogol's *Complete Works* (in Russian). St. Petersburg,
1880, vol. iii., p. 230.
[2] *Verfassung der Republik Polen.*

are generically the same in Great Russia and in Poland. The appearances that seem to confer upon Polish cities an urban existence as well developed as that of the towns of western Europe are illusive.[1] There are few genuinely Slav towns in Poland. With populations largely composed of Jews and Germans, Polish cities belong neither to the old nor to the new order of urban phenomena, but form an indescribable compound of both.

In Russia eleven cities are usually spoken of with a population of over 50,000 inhabitants. For an empire so vast as that of Russia, here is a state of things that, in the light of the urban statistics of western Europe, seems to border on the ridiculous. And when care is taken to eliminate foreign elements, urban Russia becomes more insignificant still. The population of the capital itself does not yet number a million; of its 860,000[2] inhabitants fully 100,000 are foreigners. Moscow, with a population of about 750,000, has a colony of 15,000 Germans, not to say anything of other nationalities. Odessa, with 150,000 inhabitants, is largely foreign. Kishinev, with 130,-000, Kiev, with 76,000, and Berdichev, with 55,000 are all largely Jewish and German in

---

[1] See M. Leroy Beaulieu's *L'Empire des Tsars et les Russes.*
[2] Census of 1884.

the character of their population. Of the re-
maining five "largest towns," Sarátov, with
96,000, is to some extent German; Kazan,
largely Tatar. It will be found, in fact, that
very few of the eleven towns have risen to
their present state of development save by reason of some special conditions of growth practically removing them from the list of purely
Slav cities. Tula, a city in the same category,
has the imperial gun factory, and supplies the
Russian people with their samovars. Both
Odessa and Nikoláiev owe much to their position on the Black Sea. The Volga naturally
gives local impulses to urban development in a
country practically without seaboard. Sarátov
is a conspicuous example of this kind of growth.
Samára, also a Volga "port," affords a still better illustration of conditions that distinguish
these riparian cities from towns in the interior
of Russia. Situation and foreign capital, as
well as Slav enterprise, have raised Samára
from insignificance to a position in which it
aspires to become a sort of Chicago for the
southeastern governments. Tsarítsyn, another
Volga city, owes its comparatively sudden development to the naphtha wells at Baku, as
well as to the Swedish enterprise which has
made it the great *entrepôt* of the petroleum
trade in Russia. There is, indeed, a foreign

character about most of the urban and trading activities of this part of the country. The great brewer of southeastern Russia is of German nationality. In towns like Kazan, Astrakhan, and Tsarítsyn, I found the smaller industries carried on largely by Persians, Tatars, Calmucks, and Germans. I remember seeing a whilom Frankfort shoemaker plying his awl in the shadow of a mosque. Out on the steppe, three miles from Tsarítsyn, when driving through an encampment of *khibitkas*, I encountered a German baker supplying his nomad customers with bread.

But the inherent weakness of urban life in Russia — the inability, even under the most favorable circumstances, of the pure Slav town to maintain the conditions necessary to its healthy development — is nowhere better seen than in the case of the old capital itself. Apart from its German colony, Moscow is the most genuinely Russian city that can be named. Hundreds of proverbial sayings testify to its antiquity and to the veneration in which it is held by the people. [1] " Moscow was built by the ages, Petersburg by millions," runs one. Another is the famous " Moscow, white-stoned,

[1] A highly interesting collection of proverbs and sayings relating to Moscow may be found in a little work entitled *Moskva v rodnoy poesii.* St. P., 1882.

golden-domed, loyal, loquacious, hospitable, and orthodox." In a third, the city is said to be "renowned for its virgins, its bells, and its *kalaches.*"[1] And in addition to its fame as the capital of the old Muscovite dominion, the city has the proud distinction, that even holy Kiev cannot dispute with it, of being the great heart of the national religion. In Russia alone the Moscow cult has endowed native literature with 43 poems, 34 historical works and 13 dramas and operas, all of them the work of the nation's most famous literary men. Moscow, besides being a city of churches,[2] has 816 factories, in which 74,000 workmen are employed, and enjoys the reputation of being the industrial metropolis of Russia. Yet, notwithstanding all this prestige, all these favoring circumstances, Moscow has no resources of population and no urban vitality that can justly be called its own. The number of deaths in the city every year exceeds that of the births. The resultant deficiency is more than made up by immigration, and it is by the aid of this influx from all parts of the empire that the old capital is enabled to put on an appearance of progress.[3] Moscow is

---

[1] A kind of bread roll.

[2] The proverbial number of churches in Moscow is "40 times 40," the real number about 400, exclusive of private and cemetery chapels.

[3] A similar state of things prevails in St. Petersburg.

none the less an artificial creation. Its spurious development is mainly due to habits and movements that have done little in Russia to favor lasting and healthy urban growth. It is a spectacle rather than a city, a resting-place rather than a residence, a convenient *pied à terre* for the migrant Russian far from his home on the great plain.

The conclusion is inevitable that the modern conception of city life and its concomitant activities had to be imported from without. Living under roofs did not at once naturalize it amongst the Slavs. "Every one," writes Karamzin, describing the beginning of the domiciliary period, "made a hut for himself at a little distance from his neighbors', in order that he might live the more comfortably and with the less danger." But afterwards, "beginning to feel themselves more necessary to each other, the Slavs erected their dwellings nearer together, thus bringing settlements into existence; while others, seeing fine cities in foreign countries, lost their love for the dark woods." The development of the settlement into the town was really a long and tedious process of evolution; the multiplication of the new urban phenomenon, when the beginning of town life finally appeared, was retarded by the habits of the people and by the exactions of the governors. Many centuries elapsed before any real need was felt for towns. The agriculturist, with tastes of the simplest kind, produced nothing that he did not want for his own use, and wanted nothing that he could not produce in the open plain. Side by side with his knowledge of agriculture was his expertness in all the industrial arts necessary to secure the comfort of his household. His domicile, which he could build himself, was a hive of multifarious industries that held out long against the principle of the division of labor, and are in some respects triumphant over it to this day. Clothes were manufactured at home with the same celerity as ploughs, and when laborers were needed there were always lusty sons eager to grow as many-sided in the business of life as their fathers. The town, save as a strategic point, could thus be dispensed with. On the other hand, migratory movements caused the desertion of numerous settlements and towns, and the consequent reversion of many promising urban oases to the domination of the steppe. At the end of the reign of Alexis Michaïlovich Russian hamlets and villages were still so ridiculously small that some of them had as few as ten *dvors*, or courtyards, while there were others so diminutive as to possess no more than three, two, and even one of these domestic inclosures.[1]

[1] Karamzin.

In the time of Peter, out of a population of 30,-
000,000 only 300,000 were dwellers in towns.
Later, when Catherine II. endeavored to foster
urban development, not a few of the artificial
creations of her *ukaz* soon became uninhabited,
were destroyed by fire, or reclaimed by the
larger life of the plain.   Catherine's real activity in this direction expended itself in attempts
to turn mere villages into cities, with a view to
the · ati n of seats for resident officials in-
trusoed with the carrying out of her new scheme
of local government.   Such of them as have
survived are villages to this day.

To natural causes like industry and trade no
really Russian town can be said to owe its existence.   Urban growth was mainly, almost
wholly, the result of some form of government
initiative.   In the earlier periods of the national
history towns were created for strategic purposes; later, administrative necessities called
them into being.   The scheme for the new municipal organization of 1870 mentioned five hundred and ninety-five towns.   Of these scarcely
a sixth have the character of purely industrial
centres; in almost a third occupations are partly
industrial, partly agricultural; the inhabitants
of the remainder devote themselves to agriculture, the smaller industries being carried on in
a few cases by people consigned to them by

scarcity of land. Herr Schlözer writes that " up to the middle of the ninth century no single town worthy of the name existed in the whole of northern Russia." Speaking in 1873 of the state of urban development Herr Schwanen-bach[1] said : —

" There are whole governments, such, for example, as Archangel, Olonets, Vologda, and Pensa, which, with the exception of the official capitals, have no town deserving that appellation. There are, more-over, government towns like Petrosavodsk, Pensa, Chernigov, Smolensk, that would degenerate into mere villages were the government officials from whom they take their importance removed."

The fact that this description needs no sub-stantial modification to-day shows that urban life in the north of European Russia has been all but stagnant since the ninth century.[2]

So far I have considered the town as con-trasted with the country, — compared urban phenomena in Russia with their rural surround-ings and west European prototypes. What the Russian town is intrinsically cannot easily be realized without personal experience. The insig-

---

[1] *Russische Revue,* vol. iv.

[2] Of the towns mentioned in the scheme of 1870, 27 had a popu-lation of 1000; 74 between 1000 and 2000 inhabitants; 194 between 2000 and 5000; 179 between 5000 and 10,000; 55 between 10,000 and 15,000; 35 between 15,000 and 25,000; 23 between 25,000 and 50,000; and 8 over 50,000.

nificant figure cut in the great plains by even the
larger cities is but imperfectly conveyed by mere
reminiscence or description.   Some of these
centres of population are generally lost sight
of in a walk of twenty minutes into the surrounding steppe, and their disappearance is all
the more startling to the unwary traveler because of the smoothness of the plain, and the
absence of everything capable of acting as an
obstacle to vision.   Should twilight surprise
him in his wanderings, the dimness of the landscape suggests marine openness in a very striking way.   The far-off horizon becomes the
spectator's sea-line; the city, if not gone altogether, seems a cliff long and low, with some
mimic seaport town clinging to its back; while
the lit-up cottage of the peasant charioteer
gleams from the distance like a welcome pharos
inviting belated wanderers into harbor.

Or, to offer another illustration, let the reader
accompany me in imagination for a moonlight
drive along the post road in one of the southeastern governments.   We journey for hours in
the gray glimmer, seeing nothing but sky and
plain.   All at once a few grayish, dark objects
rise up suddenly in front; the *yamshchik* calls
"*Derevnya!*" [1] and we thereupon find ourselves
entering a village by a road fully four times

---

[1] Village.

as broad as an English highway or a French *grande route*. The course may lead us in a straight line, or may have a dozen zigzag turnings in it, yet it remains of the same abnormal breadth throughout. The village itself is so vast that it takes our driver half an hour or more to wind us through it at full speed; and when at last we emerge again into the open plain the straggling collection of one-story erections in wood through which we have flitted seems immediately to sink back into the earth and disappear. Thus, if the height of the Russian city is insignificant, its extent is often immense. I have sometimes found a population of a few hundred persons spread over an area wider than that of many an English borough returning two members to Parliament. At one period, by no means very remote, European Russia the country was simply European Russia the town on a large scale. The spaces between the towns were the roads, and the Russian felt uneasy until he had traversed them from end to end. And to-day there is no *urbs* more Russian than the village that lies on the open plain, — a mere double row of houses, a domiciliary column on the march, or, at any rate, a sheltered line of migration inviting to movement. Let me add that precisely of this structure and form is the one popular thorough-

fare in all Russia, — the only thoroughfare
that has ever achieved a reputation in native
literature, namely, the Nevsky Prospect at St.
Petersburg.[1]

Russian city life has also had a migratory
character in its political aspects. Slav power
in European Russia frequently changed its centres of administration. The capital was long a
movable urban dignity. "A strange people,
these Russians!" wrote Gogol, in a playful
mood. "First they have their capital in Kiev,
but there it is too warm; then the Russian metropolis goes to Moscow, where it is not cold
enough; and finally Providence gives us St.
Petersburg."[2]   Gogol only told a part of the
truth, since, in addition to its presence at the
three cities named, the Russian capital was vir-
tually at Novgorod, Pskov and Viatka.   The
earlier selection of sites for the capital depended
mainly upon political circumstances; the choice
truer to the migrant instincts and habits of the
Russian people was the choice of St. Petersburg.
It opened a door, as well as a window, upon
Europe; it connected the Nevsky Prospect with
the thoroughfares of the settled civilizations
in the west.

A special character belongs as well to the

---

[1] See Gogol's sketch, *Nevsky Prospect.*
[2] *Peterburgskiya Zapiski.*

Russian house as to the city. Language bears
testimony to the smallness of the early residences of the Slavs, since *izba*, the word which in
Russian means a peasant's domicile, signifies in
Polish (that is to say, in a language that better
preserves the older forms of Slavonic speech
than does Great Russian) simply " room " or
" apartment." Peter's love of small rooms, his
embarrassment in spacious and high apartments,
were characteristics genuinely Slav. To this
day, moreover, the least costly dwellings are
roughly made out of forest timber by the
dweller himself ; the wooden habitations of
merchants and people of the middle class not
only lack complexity of structure, but are furnished in the simplest fashion. Beds in Russian
country houses are often mere couches, or even
drawer-holding chests covered with rugs. In
some of the best hotels they are barely broad
enough to prevent a sleeper from finding his
way to the floor. It is the custom throughout
Russia for the hirer of furnished lodgings to
supply his own bedclothes. When traveling
long distances Russians, delicate women not excepted, carry pillows with them, and use the
seat of the railway carriage as a bed. Nor is
this carelessness on the score of sleeping accommodation any mere modern trait of Russian life.
A certain George Turbernile, in a letter to Eng-

4

land "out of Moscow," in 1568, writes the following doggerel concerning the traveler in Russia:—

"He is wont to have a beares skin for his bed,
  And must instead of pillow clap his saddle to his head;
  In Russie other shift there is not to be had,
  For where the bedding is not good, the boalsters are too bad."

The rhymester then attempts an explanation :

"I mused very much what made them so to lie,
  Unless it be because the country is so hard :
  They feare by niceness of a bed theyr bodyes would be mar'd."

Pride in the house for its own sake is a sentiment almost unknown. This is why, as a rule, Russians are so careless about their domiciles, and why the domiciles so often wear a neglected look to the foreigner fresh from the west. It seems so uncommon a thing in Russia for a man to possess his own house that the language has a special phrase to express domiciliary ownership.[1] Russian servants and waiters invariably enter rooms without knocking, as if intentionally ignoring such obstacles to movement as doors.

The house of the noble, the country house of the landed proprietor, is not always a genuine Slav domicile. Not a few of its features have been borrowed from western Europe. The real Russian house must be sought far off from the sound of the French and German language — that is to say, amongst the peasantry. The

[1] "*Sobstvenny dom.*" Literally, "one's own house."

domiciles of the poorer belonging to this class
are little more than so many single rooms. I
remember, traveling through the government
of Samára, having to pass a night in a house
that at first seemed of unusually large propor-
tions, but which, on my entering, at once assumed the ordinary aspect of the Russian *izba*.
The apartment, swelled in my imagination to
an extra room, turned out to be quite empty;
the room constituting the house had for furniture a huge stove, a dozen or more broad
shelves nailed up, one over the other, to form
the bed accommodation of the household, several rudely fashioned chairs, a table, a low
wooden settle, and the *icon* frame in an angle
of the apartment. This was the dwelling-place
of three brothers, two of whom had wives and
children.

To apolism, then, as I have endeavored to
sketch this remarkable phenomenon, Russia
owes not a few of the influences by which its
civilization has been moulded. Much in the
Russian character arises from the lack of those
urban associations and activities felt and seen
in the older states of western Europe. Pride
in a profession or trade for its own sake, — the
result of that minute division of labor brought
about by high urban development, — does not
appear to exist in Russia. · In its place one no-

tices a quite realistic readiness to change one
vocation for another, side by side with remarkable aptitude for acquiring specialistic skill and
many-sidedness in necessary adaptations to new
sets of circumstances. Scientific pursuits of a
recreative character are rarely indulged in by
private persons; people with " hobbies " may
be said not to exist at all. Nor is there much
room in the native heart for the sentiment of
place. The Russian is attached to his family
and to his friends; wherever they are, there
also are his affections. But in the house, the
town, or the government in which he may
happen to reside, his interest is conspicuously
small. His domicile may be burned down in
the course of the year; his town, — and all
Russian towns are alike in this respect, — lacks
everything needed to make a centre of population attractive; while migrant habits have given
to the mere district a conception as generically
wide as that of the province itself. Between
the ardent patriotism of the Russian and the
not less warm personal affections of his home
life stretches an immense plain of colorless in-
difference.

The political consequences of apolism have,
on the other hand, been grave and far-reaching.
Nor will this seem strange, when it is remembered at what critical periods the interests of

urban development have stood in direct antagonism to the arrangements of absolute power.
In quite early times the country sacrificed its
free republics and municipal institutions to the
peculiarities of administrative centralization ; at
later epochs one finds well-meaning and enthusiastic, but unpractical, reformers, conspiring
against city growth by their very efforts to secure its promotion. Fiscal and administrative
necessities taught the wisdom of attempts at
improvement, but the imitators of the urban
institutions of the west ignored the very first
conditions of successful tinkering with the
autonomous organization of the old Slav commune. It was comparatively easy to import
forms of urban government from the west. To
erect a structure, or series of structures, that
should strike by the novelty of their outlines
and the complexity of their architecture was no
insuperable task. But to give stability and
permanence to those structures was impossible,
simply because they lacked the needed foundation in the life, habits, and traditions of the
people. [1]

[1] The latest experiment in municipal organization, that of 1870,
is still on its trial. The journal *Dyelo* pointed out in the month of
September, 1883, that only 17,751 persons, out of a population of
860,000, elect the 252 deputies for the municipal council (*duma*)
of the Russian capital. "We thus see," it proceeds, "St. Petersburg's population reduced to a mere handful, and nearly a million
people governed by a body that could easily be lodged in a single *étage* of one of our grand hotels."

The gate of the Slav city, with its rude masonry and gaudy paint, appeared only at Moscow, but it was everywhere symbolized by the yoke under which the Russians passed to the dregs of their humiliation. The despair of political subjection menaced them from every portal, and was the promise of their destiny in every land. In the west and south they pledged their allegiance to alien kings. In the east, we see their individual liberties, their local autonomies and republican federations, overridden and trampled under foot by the lust for centralization and absolute power. Prowess, courage, endurance — all the qualities necessary to the successful pursuit of war, — these the Slav never lacked. Russian epic literature is one continuous story of campaign and conquest, of military heroes and their martial exploits. From the time of their first attack on Constantinople down to the fall of Geok Tepé, or the acquisition of Merv, the Russians have never been known to show deficiency in boldness or enterprise. Slav towns were the real sources of their political weakness. •Western life, at a very early period, brought into existence a class of sturdy burghers, jealous watchers of the encroachments of sovereignty, and ready on the smallest provocation to sally forth in assertion of the rights of citizenship. Such were

the burghers of many of the English towns;
such were the burghers of Antwerp; such, indeed, were the citizens of all European towns
that had the power of free growth, and were
not cramped in their activities. It is true that
at times this burgher spirit could be humiliated; at times it was even temporarily crushed,
but it never died out of the hearts of the
urban populations. And it was this spirit, —
not to mention the commoner English examples
of its influence, — that in the Middle Ages
brought the free Italian cities into existence,
and forced from Barbarossa the famous concession of urban rights and privileges. It was
this spirit that animated the successful clamor
of the French towns in the days of Louis le
Gros. It was this spirit, in fine, that scattered
city charters all over western Europe, that almost everywhere, winning urban privilege here,
aiding municipal development there, materially helped to humanize the relations between
the governing and the governed classes. But
Russian towns, once they became entangled in
the web of which the woof was of Byzantium
and the warp from Asia, had neither free cities,
urban privileges, nor charters. From about the
middle of the thirteenth century, they existed
merely as taxable communities, without other
significance than that which the fiscal necessi-

ties of the country dictated.[1]   In Russia, under
such circumstances as these, there could be no
municipal institutions resembling those of western Europe.   The burgher spirit was entirely
wanting, and remains defective to this day.

The distance between the towns had its parallel in the distance between the people;   the
straggling, imperfect character of the former,
the migrant habits of the latter, rendered all
effective solidarity for the purposes of political
combination highly difficult, if not impossible.
In a Slav, and not a Roman sense, the Russians
were doomed to be divided and governed.   In
the towns they suffered municipal annihilation,
yet had to bear the burden of fiscal tyranny;
in the country at large, they underwent enslavement, ostensibly as cultivators of the glebe,
but really as convenient instruments of taxa-
tion.   And in the one case, as in the other,
the very conditions of their bondage were destined to continually renew in them their old
passion for liberty,— for individual rights, for
freedom of movement, and for a popular autonomous form of government.   •

[1] See writings of Dityatin on urban administration in Russia.

ENVIRONMENT.

In its climactic life Russia presents as specialized a series of phenomena as it is perhaps
possible to imagine. The severity of its extremes of heat and cold, the dryness of its
atmosphere, the facilities which its contour
gives for the diffusion of climactic changes, the
freedom of its weather from marine modification, — all these isolate it from the countries of
western Europe as completely as it is separated
from them by the conditions of its national
growth. Its seasons present the sharpest contrasts. To its brief summer of almost tropical
heat is opposed a winter of extraordinary rigor,
wherein the country loses its rivers and much
of its seaboard for six months out of every
twelve. Between the greatest heat and the
greatest cold of a single year in European
Russia, it is no uncommon thing to experience
a difference of seventy degrees centigrade. To
a "longest day" of nearly nineteen hours in
the capital is opposed in winter a day in which
the sun is scarcely six hours above the horizon.

Climactic changes, moreover, occur with characteristic abruptness. The summer ebbs out with a movement rapid as that of the retreating tide along a level shore, and almost ere one has time to say it freezes, the whole country is ice-bound. A few days is a time sufficiently long to complete even the most startling of these changes. One week rivers like the Neva and Volga may be alive with craft, the one gay with pleasure boats, the other full of freight-bearing barges; the next week they may be seen completely frozen over. This stagnation of rivers in Russia is all the more striking because of the impressiveness of its appeal to the imagination. Slav mythology, I think, fitly includes winter and death in the same personification; for Marana, the goddess of both, presides over phenomena so suggestive of ordinary mortality that, with the dying of the rivers, it is impossible not to associate the dying of animals and of men. The sudden stagnation of a living, flowing mass; the aspect of immense congealed blocks piled one upon another, or of irregular masses protruding from the surface, suggesting forces that once had free play, but have all at once been stricken with paralysis; the abnormal silence of one's progress over the snow-clad ice; the gloom of the brief day or the long glimmer of the moonless night, —

these not only convey to the mind a sense of desolation and death, but color it with a feeling of almost personal bereavement. In the Russian, at any rate, these climactic changes find a complete physiological response. His moods are no more equable than those of the weather. They often present a series of the most startling contrasts. The Russian individuality, like the Russian climate, has its winters of gloomy melancholy and pessimism, its springs of sudden hope, its summers of hot feeling and passion.

And if winter is nowhere so desolate and woe-begone in its aspects as in Russia, nowhere else, I think, is the idea of resurrection so completely realized, not only in the suddenness of the uprising, but in the effects produced by the returning warmth. On the darkest, longest night of winter, when to the experience of only a single season everything would seem hopelessly involved in the grasp of cold and darkness, there is still left a sign of life. A low note reaches the ear listening attentively near the edge of the frozen stream. This is the swash of underflowing currents; or rather, can we not say, the musical resurgam-chant of some watery Enceladus that, whatever may happen in Egypt or in Mexico, must inevitably awake at the spring? And so nowhere as in Russia is there the same inner sustenance in times of adversity, the same eagerness for renaissance, for re-birth, the same patient confidence in a something better, a something warmer and brighter, destined to arise out of the darkest and most desolate winters of the individual and the national life. How far in other countries the belief in a future existence may have been promoted by these renewals of nature cannot, perhaps, be known; but in Russia there are many evidences of the influence and of the strength of its appeal to the imagination. Without embodying any distinct conception of a future life, the old Slav faith regarded the souls of the dead as co-participants with the living in the vicissitudes of the seasons. For the departed, winter was considered a time of night; but as soon as spring returned, the soul rose to new life and enjoyment. The dead ascended from their graves at the first *prazdnik*, or fête day, of the newly-born sun; and to this hour there is a festival, coincident with that just named in point of time, which the liturgical language of the Greek Church associates with the *stranstvovaniya dukhov*, or "journeying of souls." The *russalki*, or so-called water-nymphs of Slav mythology,— those enchanting figures that still haunt the realm of poesy and picture in Russia, — are known to be nothing more, in a philological sense, than the spirits of

human beings that have arisen from the grave
to enjoy the re-birth at nature's annual renaissance.[1] Associating them with rivers in the
conception of a common re-awakening, Slav
mythology seems to have put forth its happiest
effort of imagination.

Sun worship, too, lingers amongst the Russians in interesting ways. Even after Christianity had fairly established itself in the land,
the solar myths of the old Slav nature-worship
continued to retain their hold upon the popular
mind. The same Vladimir who caused the
Pagan thunder god to be flogged and thrown
into the Dnieper came to rank amongst the
people as a sort of solar divinity. At this day
the Russian woman can say to her lover no
words more tender, more natural, or more full
of worship and admiration, than those in which
she calls him her *krásnoyĕ sólnyshko*, her
"beautiful sun." It was, of course, inevitable
that especial attention should be paid to solar
functions in a country like Russia. The long
rigorous winter, the sudden metamorphosis of
spring, give an immense significance to the periods of increasing warmth. Solar beneficence
is often acknowledged in Russian poetry. At
times one finds the acknowledgment in the form

[1] See Soloviev's *Istoriya Rossii s drevnyeishnikh Vremen.*

of personification and apostrophe. Some lines relating to events of the seventeenth century run, " Rise, O red sun, and give us warmth! We are no robbers ; we are the soldiers of Sténka Rázin." Whoever has been abroad in the Russian plain in the depth of winter, exposed to an atmosphere thirty [1] degrees below freezing point, — an atmosphere which seems to penetrate through the thickest wrappings, and turns water to ice ere it can be thrown to the ground, — will not wonder at the readiness with which the Russians see in the sun all that is glorious, life-sustaining, and bountiful. To the Slav winter is a despotism, and he witnesses its overthrow with a joy scarcely less great than that of a people welcoming the dawn of their freedom. Such, at any rate, is the testimony of church festival and folklore, of tradition and song.

The forest growths of Russia, at one time overrunning almost all the central and northern territories, must have contributed powerfully to the polytheistic faiths of the early Slavs. The rushing of the wind amongst the trees, the play of sunlight on trembling leaves, the swaying and groaning of great trunks, the storm bursting over them with its lightning flash, — every mood of the forest, from its softest whisper

[1] Réaumur.

to its loudest roar, its thousand variations of
light and ·shade, silence and sound, — all these
taught the omnipresence of deity,[1] and im-
planted it so deeply in the Slav nature that the
Russians believe in their forest spirits to this
day. True it is that the colonization of the
country, involving the disappearance of an immense number of trees, could not fail to favor
the monotheistic views of the Christian religion; yet the homeless genii of the woods, deprived of their natural habitat, continued to
live on in the imagination that gave them birth.
By atmospheric conditions alone the Russians
were marked out for tendencies towards the
superstitious in religion. Subject to a conti-
nental climate, living in a state of peculiar
nearness to natural forces, they were highly
sensitive to phenomena not visibly the result
of human agency. These atmospheric conditions of Russian development were, in fact,
analogous in several respects to those which,
in quite modern times, have favored curious
superstitions of mountainous territories, to be
found, for example, in Switzerland, the High-
lands of Scotland, and the hills of Derbyshire.

[1] The power of forests to suggest the supernatural seems proof
against all processes of civilization. Mr. Emerson mentions the
case of a lady for whom forests always appeared to *wait*, — that
is to say, to suspend a certain mysterious life until after the passage of the intruder.

Even in New England, with its severe and variable climate, religion has a highly spiritual character, a strong super-sensual element, betraying the influence of conditions that do not exist, or that exist to a much less degree, in the mother country. In another way, too, does hill life help the conservation of superstitious terrors. It separates people instead of bringing them together. It weakens a community's sense of numbers, its feeling of nearness, its consciousness of solidarity and strength. This is, no doubt, why civilization made so much and such rapid progress in Europe, which of all the quarters of the world has the lowest mean altitude. It is true that Russia had no mountains, but her people were separated very effectively by geographical, ethnic and political causes. And Russian civilization came so late that before the eighteenth century the country had no literature at all worthy of the name.[1]

The political effects of climate upon Russian development must have been considerable. In some quarters it has been suggested that extreme cold prepared the Slavs for the Mongol yoke and the autocracy which came after it.[2] It is just as probable that extreme heat, by making people indolent, directly favors abso-

---

[1] Russia's first poet was Lomonosov, born 1711 ; died 1760.
[2] M. A. Leroy Beaulieu.

lute government and the usurpation of power, — a relation of cause to effect often illustrated in the history of eastern and southern peoples. If climate be recognized as one of the factors of national growth, it will be found that far more people have been enslaved or deprived of their liberties through the influence of extreme heat than owing to that of excessive cold. A moderate degree of cold has always been favorable rather than injurious to civilization. It braces the physical system, and permits a high degree of mental activity. I must, therefore, describe the Russian winter as having been the enemy rather than the friend of Mongolism in all its forms. Cold has a special as well as a general way of aiding a nation's intellectual growth ; it induces reflective habits ; it favors the tendency of a monotonous landscape to throw the mind back upon itself. Under the influence of cold, faculties deprived of exterior sources of interest, unable to assimilate and convert into ideas impressions not satisfactory to the mind, all the more eagerly seek interior or reflective occupation. Hence, the Russian intellect is subjective rather than objective, reflective rather than observational, analytic rather than descriptive. While they have done much as a race for science, I have not been able to find Russians remarkable for proficiency in

5

anything that exacts highly-developed descriptive powers, or close attention to the minute in nature. A west European novelist having domiciliary business with one of his characters will often describe a whole house, from ground floor to ceiling, not omitting the minutest or the most multipedalian detail. Russian writers may picture, but they rarely describe. Pisemsky wrote whole novels without a line of description. Even in the descriptions of Gogol, who wrote in Great Russian, but was a Little Russian at heart, a strong subjective element may be detected. Some of the most striking of Turgeniev's books contain very few descriptive passages. The descriptions of recent " peasant literature " in Russia are the result of borrowed habit, or of the ethical purposes of certain modern schools. Among Russian translators it is very common to shorten or wholly omit descriptive passages from west European novels. During the recent war between Russia and Turkey quite a sensation was created in the former country by the publication of long descriptive reports translated from the London " Daily News."

The Russians excel, on the other hand, in everything that exacts wide views, broad generalizations. Their talent for philosophical speculation is, considering all the circumstances of the case, remarkably large. It seems to manifest itself in every department of intellectual activity. Russian poetry revealed the reflective tendency in the earliest youth of Russian literature. Lomonosov, whom Aksakov, the Slavophil writer and critic, describes as "the one true source of all the Russians have accomplished, are accomplishing, or shall accomplish in the field of literary activity," was as much philosopher as poet.. It was he who delivered a celebrated discourse on the origin of light, and out of such material as "the uses of glass" produced the first, and, as is frequently alleged, the best, didactic poem in the Russian language. It was Lomonosov who, long before the breaking out of the *Kulturkampf* between science and theology in Western Europe, proclaimed that "science and faith are sisters, the offspring of one mighty parent; nor can there ever arise real dissension between the two." It was Lomonosov who said that "the man who thinks he can learn astronomy or chemistry from his psalter is no more a true theologian than he is a true philosopher who imagines that with a mathematical line he can measure the divine will." Russian art, too, is a Janus with two faces, one of them imitative in its aspirations, the other "sicklied o'er with the pale cast of thought." Russian pictures have a peculiar sug-

gestiveness apart from the fidelity of their rep-
resentations. This tendency seems to reach
its fullest and most successful expression in
Vereshchagin, whose paintings are genuine phi-
losophies, whose appeal is to the reflective, and
through them to the emotional faculties.[1] States-
manship, diplomacy, and officialism also have
their reflective side in Russia. Exceedingly
abstract philosophical propositions occasionally
find their way into state papers and public reports. In the schools and educational establishments — not only in professors' lectures, but in
the essays of pupils — the same tendency is displayed of the Russian mind to occupy itself
more with categories than with single facts,
more with generalizations than with details,
more with principles than with things.[2]

Thus far I have spoken only of climactic environment. There still remain for consideration the material surroundings of Russian life
— the character of its objective world as cog-
nized, to use a philosophical expression, through
the organs of vision. The monotonousness of

[1] I refer mainly, of course, to Vereshchagin's celebrated illustrations of the Russo-Turkish War, such as Our Wounded, After
the Attack, Prisoners, All Well in the Shipka Pass, etc.

[2] I remember once applying to a Russian library official for the
"main facts in the life and literary activity of Pissarev." The result was a manuscript discussing the "significance" of Pissarev as
the founder of the "art school," and his relation to Bielinsky,
founder of the "æsthetic school."

the Russian landscape is well known. It is true that, traveling in bright weather through some parts of the country, one has glimpses of villages with their gold-capped churches, or of water-courses glittering in the sunlight, or of the flash of scythes in distant harvest fields. Moments like these are like the rare smile of the sickly invalid rather than the perpetual cheerfulness of robust health. There is no real picturesqueness in Russian scenery. Even the waving steppes, luxuriant of life as they are and full of flowers, have something mournful and pathetic about them that may be felt, but can never be adequately expressed. Russians love the scenery of their native land with the same kind of affection as that which parents lavish upon a consumptive child ; and if these fertile steppes seem to show more color than may be found in other parts of Russia, it is only because they are for moments aglow with the hectic flush, the fever light of the Russian life and environment. Much darker is the picture presented by the woodlands ; these combine the wild disorder and luxuriance of Russian vegetation in all its arboreal forms. Immense tracts of mere brushwood sometimes stretch to the horizon, or the prospect is darkened by sweeps of moorland equally vast, without shrub, or bush, or tree. Elsewhere, broad, ochre-tinted patches

mark where the communal land is under cultivation.   But the long, wide plains of a mournful, deadened green exert a depressing influence
upon the mind, and the eye wanders willingly
for relief to the far-off march of some forest
tract closing in the monotony with a band of
sombre brown.

Portions of European Russia are wild and
desolate in the extreme.   Along the lower
Volga one may journey for fifteen miles without seeing a single habitation.   The "stations"
are merely oases of wood lost in vast stretches
of steppeland void of vegetation.   On each side
the country extends bare and level as far as the
horizon, and if snow enters the prospect, as it
did for me, the dull, blinding monotony of the
spectacle becomes almost unbearable.

The same beggarliness and impoverishment
characterize the exterior aspects of village life
in the provinces.   The impression they make
is well suggested by Pushkin's satirical picture :

"Admire the view before us — that wretched row of huts;
Behind them a long and level descent of black land,
Above them a thick bank of grayish clouds.
Where are the gay fields ?   Where the shady woods ?
Where the river ?   In the yard there, near the fence,
Shoot up two miserable trees to glad the eye —
Just two and no more; and of them one has been
Shorn by autumn rains of every beauty;
While the sparse leaves on the other are withered and yellow,
Awaiting the first breeze to fall and putrefy
The sluggish pond below."

.And if Russian out-door life in the country has no hedge-rows or flower gardens to make it attractive, the Russian town is equally deficient in picturesqueness. If, on the one hand, there are no ivy-clad ruins to meet the eye with their pleasant suggestions, there is, on the other, a marked absence of beauty in all the forms of architectural design. If it were to be suddenly discovered that the cathedral at Cologne were a mere piece of elaborate wood-carving, the impression that splendid structure now makes upon admirers would be felt no more; and so the most fancifully shaped domicile of urban Russia is at best but a structure of wood. Most of these houses are rude rather than ornamental in their outlines; to the eye of the traveler they are a source of continual weariness. Dirty streets, carts mud-colored as the domiciles themselves, the soiled and torn habits of migrant or beggar peasants, the continual cloud of dust raised in warm weather by the wind, — all these intensify the depressing influences of the Russian environment, giving it a sameness that seems to pervade everything, animate and inanimate.

The exceptions do little more than prove the rule. I am bound to admit that from the high tower of Ivan Veliky, right in the thick of the churches and palaces of the Kreml, the view to

be had of Moscow is striking. The eye rests,
or rather wanders, over a vast panorama of
house-tops painted red and green; here and
there dazzling gilded cupolas shine in the sun.
But this kind of picturesqueness is rather the
rash extreme of tastes fed perpetually on the
monotonous than the calmly studied contri-
vance of a people born into an environment of
cheerful coloring and contour. Taking this
view of the matter one may see in the Russian
peasant's liking for a red shirt the same search
for contrast as that which, in the villages, sometimes leads a man to paint his house in glaring
colors, or in the cities impels him to provide
his shop with a ludicrously gaudy signboard.[1]

Pretty women, travelers often say, are scarce
in Russia. This is only another way of stating
the extent to which Russian women have suffered from the imbruting labor of the fields,
from the long confinement of the *terem*, from
the domestic slavery of the wife, from the late
and only partial advent of modern comforts,
luxuries, and refinements to the Russian home;
yet environment has also done its part in help-
ing to make feminine beauty somewhat scarce
in Russia. For centuries the race has been
looking out over wide, formless plains. Nature
gave it no ideals of beauty, nor, until a period

[1] A common habit in St. Petersburg.

comparatively recent, did art. Its efforts at
ornamentation long linked it with the gaudy
exaggerations of barbarism. And to this day
its church pictures and icons are mere repre-
sentations of sallow-faced, melancholy-visaged
saints wasted by persistent mortification of the
flesh.

I speak thus with reference to the people
as a whole. Peasants are peasant-like; and in
an empire of them it would be too much to
look for a beauty at every turn. Of the men I
can only say that in countenance and physique
their superiority over the English and west European Hodge is indisputable. Some of these
inland Slavs, with their regular features and
flowing beards, would tempt many a painter in
Paris or Rome from his artisan model. When
traveling through the Tambov government I
saw many really beautiful "Christ heads"
amongst the peasants. The Russian country
woman, on the other hand, is generally "plain"
of feature, yet not nearly so wanting in interest
as it has been the habit of foreign prejudice to
represent. Blooming cheeks are impossible in
a dry atmosphere like that of Russia. *En re-
vanche,* the Slav woman displays two rows of
white teeth that would almost make a west-
European rival die of jealousy. She is not
cramped by her dress, and has a natural dignity

and grace of movement that might be envied,
yet not easily imitated elsewhere.   Nekrassov
writes : —

> "In many a Russian village we may find such women,
> With quiet earnestness of face,
> With the grace of strength in every movement
> As they go by with regal gait and queenly mien."

Amongst the educated classes of the towns,
moreover, the Russian woman is not less frequently pretty and much oftener attractive than
is the woman of the west.

But there was another tendency, to the forming of which environment must have made large
contributions.   Missing color, variety, perfection
of form, beauty of feature, in his own surroundings, the Russian all the more readily went
elsewhere in search of the picturesque.   The
very custom of living in houses seems to have
been suggested to the Slavs by the experiences
and sight-seeing of their travelers in foreign
countries.   And when the habit of going abroad
became established amongst certain classes of
the people, traveled Russia would not fail to
grow somewhat tired of its environment, or at
least desirous of importing into its surroundings
— intellectual as well as material — certain influences of modification.   But as only a favored
few could go abroad, this tendency would take a
passive form amongst the masses, and hence

would develop itself that taste for the foreign which found its fullest expression in 'Peter and is at this day one of the most striking of all the characteristics of the Russian Slavs. Only when it threatened political injury or social grievance did the outlandish fall into disrepute; for the people came at last to draw a marked distinction between acts of predilection like that which imported autocracy from Byzantium and those that merely gave an Italian architect to the Vassily-Blagennoy Church, or filled the courts of Tsars and Tsarítsas with adventurers of Dutch, German, and French nationality.

OLD RUSSIAN LIFE.

HAVING thus glanced at the more important of the permanent influences that have directed the course of Russian development, — notably those of habit and environment, — we may now consider the political and religious causes which at a very early period completely reshaped the destinies of the Russian people. Of all the influences that helped to mould the national development, by far the most significant and far-reaching in their consequences were the changes by which, on the one hand, Russia accepted the religion of the Greek Church and on the other bowed her neck to Mongol rule during nearly two centuries of enslavement and humiliation. What the nation lost and what it gained from these foreign systems of worship and politics will be best seen by comparing the early Russia of pagan faith with the middle Russia, upon which the Tatar oppressors, at last ejected from Slav soil, had left the indelible marks of their influence. And here the question to be answered is not so much whether

the changes wrought were politically expedient
or even inevitable, or on the whole a good compromise between the evils and advantages present alike in two systems, but whether they
were calculated to suit the habits and traditions
of the people, whether they caused inroads into
customs and liberties deep-rooted in the national
genius; whether they made life freer, happier,
and more comfortable for the Russian Slav, or
whether they were destined to plant in the
racial and individual consciousness the seeds of
an eternal discontent. For the purposes of such
an inquiry I propose to divide Russian history
into three great natural periods. The first of
them terminates with the forcible conversion of
the Russians to the Greek faith (972-1015);
the second includes the whole formative period
of Byzantine and Tatar influence up to the
beginning of Peter's reign; in the third may be
included Russian development from the early
years of the eighteenth century down to our own
times. We shall thus see the purely Slav period of Russian history, the national life as it
was moulded by Greek and Mongol influences,
and the Russia of modern times, Europeanized
in detail, yet left as Asian in structure as when
it fell to the grand princes of Moscow from the
hands of the Mongol Khans.

In the domain of religion the early Russians

must have suffered all the disadvantages which, in modern times, are associated with a " pagan " faith. Without any system of rewards and punishments, no prospect of comfort in the next world tempted them to well-doing in this. But there was one idea which lay deep in the imagination of the Slav, and which is still there at this day despite all the efforts of Christianity to uproot it. The early Russians, in place of the modern conception of a future life, not only believed in the continued existence of the souls of men after death, but held it possible to have intercourse with them. To the existence of this faith the old songs and burial lamentations of the north of Russia bear abundant testimony. " The bright red sun," [1] runs one of them, "has hidden itself behind high mountains and wintry clouds ; it leaves me, poor wretch that I am, alone with my children." But after the death of a husband, it was the custom for the widow to throw herself upon his grave.[2] There, mourning, she confesses she has forgotten to ask where she must await her spouse. If he will return to her, let him say whether he will come at midnight, in the clear moonlight, or at noon when the sun is shining, or in the early morning, or late at night. If he will come at night she will

[1] That is, the departed, the deceased.

[2] See *Prichitanya Syevernavo Kraya*, by E. B. Barsovym. Moscow, 1872.

have everything ready for his visit; she will put her children to sleep and will sit beside the window waiting for him. "Whether thou comest as a gray hare out of the bush or as an ermelin from behind the stone, I shall not be afraid. I shall receive thee. Come in the old way, as was thy wont. Be here again the father of the household and the chief." Sometimes a small house was built over the grave in the belief that the deceased would return and inhabit it. At the dinner following the interment a vacant chair was left for the departed, and on the table before it the guests spilled food. Even after the introduction of the Christian worship it was long a habit for the relatives to invite the priest to the house on the fortieth day after the burial, it being supposed that the dead member of the family would accompany him. Occasionally the priest was induced to pass a night in the domicile; in which case there was added to the furniture of his sleeping room a spare bed, wherein, it was believed, the deceased would also spend several hours in slumber. The old Russians had a habit of visiting their dead in the churchyard, whence the word for burial ground, *pogosta*, derived from *gost*, or guest, host. Even at the present day, on the occasion of certain festivals, crowds flock to churchyards and cemeteries, carrying with them drinks and food of various kinds, to be eaten from the gravestones, which are used as tables. Feasting in this way, the people believe that they are brought into close communion with the dead. Hence, on the whole, paganism was not without a certain consolation. But the great merit of the old Slav faith in the eyes of Russians was of a negative rather than of a positive character. It brought no narrow asceticism or ecclesiastical prohibition to cramp the heart and chill the soul, to brand with criminality the most harmless pleasures, and in a panic fear, born of dogma and narrowness, to make delight in existence for its own sake seem a crime rather than a blessing. Nor did it aid in ruining the free republics, in destroying the liberties of the people, in weakening the sense of individual freedom, in promoting the aims of autocratic power.

The manners of the early Russians have not always been depicted in the most favorable light. Yet it is noteworthy that disparaging accounts of them had their origin in a source not unlikely to be influenced by prejudice. The monk Nestor wrote as a zealous Christian would naturally write of pagans. His testimony lacks corroboration in some essential particulars; even if accepted implicitly it does not show that the Russians were in a condition at all worse than

that of other tribes and races from whose horizon the glimmerings of civilization were yet far
off. Yet even Nestor makes an exception in
favor of the Polyans,[1] while amongst the Slavyans [1] customs prevailed which distance, in their
generosity and philanthropic feeling, the most
altruistic inspirations of the Christian faith.
To these untutored children of the plain and
the forest the traveler or wanderer was a being
of peculiar sanctity — a holy man worthy to be
worshiped. They received him with caresses,
and took pride in lodging him and supplying
his needs with the best of that which they had.
Neglect to protect him from evil and misfortune
of all kinds was regarded as a breach of the
rude social order that prevailed in those early
times ; so important, in fact, was this duty of
hospitality that, to discharge it, even theft was
considered lawful. That is to say, if a man
had no means of entertaining a guest, he was
entitled to obtain them from his richer neighbor.
The Slavyan often left his door open, and food
spread ready in the domicile, in order that
the *strannik*, or traveler, might enter freely and
eat.[2]

Now, if it be true, as we are constantly told,
that altruism is but a higher form of egotism, it
is quite possible that some utilitarian motives

---

[1] Tribes of the early Slavs.   [2] See Karamzin.

lay at the bottom of these hospitable customs
of the early Slavs. A religious superstition —
some vaguely felt reflex of the old belief that
deities walked the earth at times in the garb of
beggars and of travelers — may have invested
the wanderer with that sanctity which the early
Russian attached to his person and condition.
Even so late as the beginning of the eighteenth
century we find a writer of didactic literature,
one Ivan Possoshkov, teaching that beggars are
the representatives of God, and that unless they
are treated well God will be angry.[1] On the
other hand, a traveler had seen much, and was
likely to bring with him a fund of interesting information concerning distant cities, or even foreign countries. The desire of being well spoken
of was also a possible motive for the kindly
treatment of strangers. In Vladimir's advice to
his sons, — a twelfth century document, — that
prince's children were charged to receive strangers hospitably, " because," runs the text, " they
have it in their power to give you a good or a
bad reputation." Admitting the plausibleness
of all these considerations, there still remains
in the hospitality of the early Russians an altruistic, a philanthropic element that cannot be
explained by referring it to gross egotistical

---

[1] Compare Nausicaä's saying in the Odyssey, "Strangers and
the poor are the messengers of the gods."

motives. This is shown in the characteristics of the old racial virtue as it survives in Russia to this day. No treatment of the modern *strannik* surpasses in kindliness and disinterestedness that which is lavished upon the traveler constrained to throw himself upon the hospitality of the eastern Slav. I have received attentions from wandering Tatars, and have had whole nights made comfortable for me by pastoral Calmucks, yet I have never fallen asleep lulled into slumber by such a delicious sense of the tender solicitude of strangers as when, belated, I have had to seek temporary shelter in the rude dwelling of a Russian peasant. Methinks Dazh-bog, the sun-god, were he to wander to-day into the hut of the *muzhik*, disguised as a man, could meet there with no better treatment than that which is ungrudgingly, nay gladly, bestowed upon the genuine mortal. Remember, moreover, that this hospitality is its own reward. You pay the dispenser neither in stories, nor in praise, nor in money. Hence it may be pertinent to ask, with such a mere survival before us, what must this Slav virtue have been in the days of its strength?

For characteristics and conceptions innate in the national and individual consciousness of the Russian Slav, we must look to the *bwyliny*, the epic songs of the people, as they were chanted before the coming of the Mongols. One of the most striking of these productions personifies the national character in its hero. Ilya Muromets lives with his parents in the village of Karachov. Lame in both hands and feet, he sits behind the stove for thirty years. But one day he is visited by Christ and two apostles, disguised as travelers. These restore him to health and confer upon him heroic qualities. The *bwylina* recounts the story of his subsequent wandering and exploits. Ilya delights in reflecting that he is no knight or prince, but simply a peasant; this character he persists in maintaining to the end. Political or social ambition he has none. Ilya is a practical humanitarian. When fallen upon by robbers, instead of killing them, he splits an oak tree with a shaft from his bow, compelling the admiration of his assailants, who vainly endeavor to persuade him to become their chief. At the taking of Chernigov he refuses to put the population to the sword. When Vladimir, his prince, sends a man to certain death in war, in order that, like David, he may obtain possession of the bereaved widow, Ilya reproaches him for the cowardly deed. A quarrel ensues, and the two are long estranged. Yet the prince has need of Ilya; and when the hero's services are necessary to save the nation, Ilya forgets all the insults

and ingratitude heaped upon him. Vladimir is
represented as calling upon him, with a sum-
mons in these words: "I beg thee to save the
land, not for my sake, not for my wife's sake,
not for the sake of the churches or the monas-
teries, but for the sake of the widows and the
little children." At first there is a little re-
monstrance. The long pent-up indignation finds
an outlet in reproach: "Why hast thou so long
forbidden me the road to Kiev?" The prince
repeats his entreaty; gradually the hero's heart
is gained; he forgets his wrongs, and sets out
to save the nation. It is characteristic of Ilya
that, for patriotic services of this kind, he de-
clines all reward, even refuses presents offered
to him by the prince. And Ilya's traits of pity,
gentleness, kindness, and mercy are not confined to one *bwylina* alone, but find a certain
expression in nearly all the early epic songs.
Of delight in cruelty for cruelty's sake, there
are few traces; when the Russian epic displays
deeds of bloodshed, it mentions them rather as
necessary than as capricious acts; the general
·impression conveyed associates them with coarse
and rude manners rather than with malicious
bloodthirstiness. In one song it is said that no
one exceeds Vladimir in happiness, Ilya in giant
strength, Alesha in recklessness, Dobrynya in
wisdom, Potok in beauty, Dunai in eloquence,

Duk in riches, or Kirilo in grace. There is no glorification of cruelty here.[1]

The constituent molecule of all early Russian life, social as well as political, was the freedom of the individual, an intense consciousness of personal worth, a racial tenaciousness of personal rights. Karamzin tells us that the Russian Slavs "tolerated neither rulers nor slaves," and believed in "a wild[2] and boundless liberty" as the chief good of humanity. Thus, in the early Russian epos, we find expressed, as a fundamental principle underlying all thought, action, and relationship, the most complete freedom of the individual. Even when a certain political organization became necessary, the Slavs did not abate one jot of their personal rights. In times of emergency, members of a tribe consulted with each other on a footing of the most perfect equality; and if, at these conferences, some were singled out for special deference, the tribute was paid to age, to eloquence, or to warlike qualities. The Slav family, of which the father was the natural head, had patriarchal customs and conceptions at its foun-

[1] In the Ilya story, not having the original before me, I have followed M. Viskovatov's account.

[2] Karamzin, in a moral sketch, entitled *Martha, or the Mayor's Wife*, endeavored to prove that "political order can only exist where absolute power has been established." This throws not a little light on Karamzin's prejudices as a historian.

dation. The *mir*, or commune, securing joint possession of land to the whole people, was the family on a large scale; it had a council, or *veché*, in which each household was represented. The *volost* was a union of communes, with a governing body or council formed of the elders of the *mirs*. In times of danger it was customary for the *volosti* of a tribe to appoint a chief; but these functions of headship were purely temporary. The people carefully guarded against investing one of their number with anything like permanent authority. Even when merged in the larger organization of the *volost* the commune retained all the liberties which belonged to it. As in the earlier and ruder conferences, the people continued to discuss public affairs on an equal footing. They had the same voice in dismissing as in appointing their temporary chieftains. After a time a custom arose of nominating a head from the elders of the families of a tribe. But the first real change in this highly popular and democratic form of government only took place when the Slavs of the Ilmen called in the Varegs to rule over them. Looking at the character of these Scandinavian adventurers, — at their warlike manners and capacity in military administration, — one is prepared to see the democratic government of the Slavs yield up its essential features to the political dogmas of the new-comers. Instead of mere elders, princes now wielded the sovereignty of the people. Yet the new system left Russian liberties untouched. The people, as Karamzin says, continued to maintain their communal institutions. The *veché* remained to the inhabitants of the towns, who assembled from time to time for the discussion of public affairs. The chiefs, or head-men, civil and military, were elected, not by the prince, but by the people, who chose and dismissed their ruler as before, sometimes meeting to punish him for his misconduct by a sentence of banishment.[1] The Vareg prince, in fact, took his place in the Russian political system as an administrator, rather than as a ruler; as a public servant holding his position by title of good behavior, rather than as a master claiming it as an hereditary right that could be maintained by force of arms.

Under the rule of princes, some of the Slav towns attained to considerable political distinction as republics. Such were Novgorod, Viatka, and Pskov. In each of these centres the rights of the people were insisted upon and conserved with great jealousy. Five times did the Novgorodians change their rulers in the space of seven years; and, in order to set bounds to the

[1] This happened at Pskov and Novgorod.

power of the prince and of his armed retainers,
known as the *druzhina*, the citizens compelled
their chief to promise, on oath, a strict observ-
ance of their privileges. The prince could not
become possessed of villages in the territory
over which he ruled. In harvesting and hunting he had to submit to restrictions limiting
him to certain times of the year. Below the
prince was the *possadnik*, or mayor, whose ten-
ure of office seems to have been no more certain
than that of his superior. The real rulers were
the people; for, before the prince could take
important action, he had to obtain their consent
in *veché* assembled. In addition to Viatka and
Pskov, towns like Polotsk, Smolensk, and Rostov had popular councils of this kind. The
smaller villages and settlements submitted to
the guidance of the town populations. Novgorod, moreover, enjoyed a spiritual, as well as a
political independence. After the introduction
of Christianity, the *veché* of the republic appointed its own archbishop. Such, in fact,
was the democratic and uncompromising spirit
of these free communities that later, in face
of the Tatar domination, the people rose in
rebellion against Mongol tax collectors, or murdered their *possadnik* for daring to suggest the
wisdom of a compromise with the foe.

Of early Russian legislation little is known.

The unwritten code in use prior to the coming
of the Varegs must have been of a rude and
ready kind, in harmony with the crudity of
early Russian civilization. But of its embodi-
ment of principles afterwards formally expressed in historical documents, there can be
no doubt whatever. The Russians never wholly
surrendered themselves to the foreign influences
they were from time to time compelled to in-
voke. If they accepted the rule of Scandinavian princes, they preserved intact, as long as
moral resistance and armed protest were of
avail, all their individual and communal liberties. The Slav *mir* has maintained itself
through all the vicissitudes of Russian history
to this day. The Russian spirit has survived
in every mingling of native with Asiatic races.
Hence we are justified in assuming that the
first Russian code of laws, — the *Russkaya
Pravda*,[1] — though drawn up under Scandinavian influence, preserved the spirit of Russian
law as it existed prior to the coming of the
Varegs in the ninth century. In the character
of the code itself, this assumption meets with
the strongest support. Its ruling trait is humanitarianism, — the humanitarianism of Ilya,
of the Slav epic, of the Russian nature uncor-
rupted by the dangers and temptations of

[1] Reign of Yaroslav (1016–1054).

power. Of criminal law, as it is understood in modern times, the code contains scarcely a trace. Public prisons were unknown. No legal sanction was given to corporal punishment, nor were tortures practiced to induce confessions, or debtors beaten because of their poverty. It was the signal glory of Russia in her rudest days that she refused to subscribe to the barbarous doctrine that the taking of one life necessarily demands the extinction of another, [1] and was equally remiss in carrying to its logical conclusion the not less barbarous practice of making collective murder a glorious virtue and private murder an offense worthy of the deepest execration.

In this first period of their history the Russians thus enjoyed what, in a political sense, we are fairly entitled to regard as the golden age of their national existence. As free individuals they ruled themselves. Not only had each citizen or each agriculturist a voice in the management of public affairs: his influence was as direct as his resolve was final. No complex machinery deranged the popular will, or changed its direction, or scattered its energies ; no prince, or *possadnik*, or *ataman*, dared veto the decisions of the *veché*. It was from a picturesque

---

[1] At this day capital punishment exists in Russia only for political murder.

point of view the grandest, from an administrative point of view the simplest, and from a moral point of view the most equitable form of government ever devised by man. And to-day, though the *veché* lives on, a mere shadow of its former self, quite divorced from political administration, and engaged, instead of in the business of the nation, in discussing crops, harvests, and the raising of the communal tax, it still embodies the same intolerance of sovereignty as that which characterized the early Slavs. So when an old chronicler,[1] alluding to the temper of the Russians, said of them, "Neminem ferant imperatorem," he was describing that ineradicable spirit of antipathy to encroachments upon individual and popular liberties which lies at the root of all political discontent in Russia, and which in that country makes any compromise with the principle of autocratic rule radically and permanently impossible.

[1] Cited in Karamzin's notes, vol. i.

BYZANTINISM AND THE THREE UNITIES.

THE Russia upon which our glance fell in the last chapter was the Russia of the eastern Slavs; the Russia in which the racial tendencies of the people had still free play; the Russia which had bowed its neck to no tyranny, system or principle; the Russia in which individuals and communities alike held within their grasp that most sacred of all possessions, liberty. But the Russia upon which we are now about to look is a new Russia, a Russia so metamorphosed that one can scarcely recognize it to be the same; a Russia blighted into asceticism by religion, humiliated and debased by enslavement, and finally handed over to the cupidities and tyrannies of absolute power. So rude and sudden a change was perhaps never before known in the history of national vicissitudes; one so grave and far reaching in its consequences has fallen to the lot of no other country. It long crushed the Slav spirit; it brought to a standstill almost all the racial tendencies. It was the damming-up of that great stream of national life that was one day to overflow its banks in a wide devastation.

The two events that for seven centuries of Russian history reduce every other occurrence in the national life to an almost absolute insignificance were the conversion of the people to Christianity and their enslavement by the Tatar Mongols. Essentially distinct in their character, separated from each other not only by three centuries in point of time, but also by that immense interval which stood between the barbarism of Asia and the culture of Byzantium, the two influences were yet so closely related in their effects that to the student of Russian history they must ever seem rather the elements of a subtle union, devised for the accomplishment of a common aim, than any mere fortuitous concurrence of forces at once separate and dissimilar. In some sort the Tatars may be said to have completed the work begun by the Greek Church. If from Constantinople the priests brought to Kiev the idea of a political autocracy, the Tatar Khans materially helped to weld the scattered elements of government into a centralized administration. If Byzantium contributed the conception of a unified state, Saraï[1] taught

[2] I need scarcely remind the reader that Sarai was not only the seat of Tatar dominion in Russia, but the place of pilgrimage for the subject princes.

an easy way of raising money for its expenses. So completely at times are the two influences interwoven that to decide always what was the result of Greek ecclesiasticism, and what the effect of the Tatar domination, would be a task not only difficult, but unnecessary. In some cases, nevertheless, the result is distinctly traceable to the cause.

Let us first consider the changes wrought or enforced in the manners of the people by Byzantine ecclesiasticism. Concerning these a large store of information has been preserved in that already cited document, the "Domostroï," or household guide, the composition of one Sylvester, church dignitary, and counselor of Ivan the Terrible. In this composition we find reflected not only the injunctions and prohibitions of the Greek Church, but also the actual attitude of the people towards almost every possible problem of conduct, private and public, that the ingenuity of the time could suggest. Some traits of the "Domostroï" are undoubtedly humanitarian in their character. It enjoined the people to show kindness to the poor, and to make presents of money and food to those in prison. Certain practices of cleanliness and morality were also inculcated. But the general effect of the new religious influences was to turn Russia into a vast monastery, full of fasting, penance-doing, and mortification of the flesh.[1] And though Greek, like Roman, Christianity placed its ban upon the most innocent enjoyments of life, no wave of Puritanism ever swept over the west of Europe with so deadening an effect upon the heart and the imagination as that exerted in the East by the gloomy flood of Byzantine monasticism which is seen depicted in the "Domostroï." It seemed as if the priests of the new faith, beginning with a gospel of renunciation, at last sought to bring their task to its climax by teaching the criminality of life itself. They were not content with forbidding horse-racing, hunting, and dice-playing ; the Church condemned music and musical instruments of all kinds ; it taught that even laughing was a sin. For a single member of the household to commit the crime of dancing or singing was to prepare the whole family for eternal torments in hell. Even so late as the beginning of the eighteenth century it was considered a sin for a father to allow a child in play to take him by the beard. All intercourse between the young of the two sexes was forbidden. "The youth," says Ivan Possoshkov, "must be taken to account for every idle word he speaks."

---

[1] See *Opwyt istoriko-literaturnavo Islyedovaniya o Proiskhozhdenii Drevnorusskavo Domostroya*, I. S. Nekrassova. Moskva, 1872.

The political influence wielded from the moment of its appearance in Russia by the Greek Church was one antagonistic to Slav methods of public life and government. The national system had the freedom of the individual as its foundation. Upon this rested the liberties of the communes and the towns, the privileges of the Slav republics, the free will of the people in the choice and dismissal of their ruler, and in the settlement of all public affairs. The organization of the Russian country was that of the *rod*, the tribe or family on a large scale, the prince ruling as an administrator and transmitting his appanages to his children. Here was a purely democratic form of government. It was this which the Greek Church attacked at its very foundation. The ideal brought to Russia by Byzantine priests was one in which the individual should count as nothing, and the ruler as the be-all and the end-all of the new state. Just as that ideal had replaced the many gods of the Slav polytheism by a single divinity, so it aimed at gathering the scattered potentialities of princely rule into the hands of a single Christian Cæsar, the type of the monarchs of Constantinople. And if the deities of the woods and rivers, of the earth and sea and air could so readily yield up their territories to the sway of the monotheistic God, church dignitaries naturally argued that it would be just as easy to familiarize the people with the conception of an earthly ruler having dominion, not over one *rod* alone, but over all the branches of the eastern Slavs. Gradually, if not simultaneously, Byzantine Christianity promulgated in Russia the three ideas of unity in deity, unity in sovereignty, and unity in territory. The victory of monotheism, secured by force, proved easy. For a time the old method of government maintained itself intact. But as Byzantine ideas, strengthened in their influence by appeals to the religious emotions, became predominant, the princes began to take more ambitious views of their functions as rulers. Instead of dividing the appanages amongst their children, we now see them bequeathing patrimonies to their political successors. In the fierce struggle which follows, for the preservation of power on the one hand, for the accumulation of power on the other, the grand princes of Moscow, aided by wealth acquired as financial agents of the Tatar Khans, win undisputed supremacy over their rivals. In the fifteenth century, under Ivan III., the work of territorial unification is accomplished and the country sees the end of the Mongol domination. A few decades later Ivan IV. assumes the title of Tsar. In 1547, Russia has unity in deity, unity in territory, and unity in sovereignty. The Byzantine ideas have triumphed.

But what was the price paid by Russia for the principles of autocracy and centralization? Two interesting correlations of cause and effect meet us at the outset. As long as Russian government retained its simple, patriarchal character, the necessities of the state were small and easily supplied. As long as Russian rulers were only the servants of the people, the privileges of the *vechés* remained intact, the freedom of the individual underwent no curtailment. But the moment the princes began to aim at the Byzantine type of state, that moment the old methods of raising money became inadequate. As soon as governors sought to override rather than obey the popular will, so soon were the first attacks made upon individual and communal freedom. And just as surely as Russia moved in the direction of unity and of autocracy, so surely did she create for herself embarrassments that were to find their relief in but a single kind of remedy, namely, the debasement of the people. The Mongol domination taught the princes the double art of amassing wealth and accumulating power. In the new government the individual fell from the status of a free personality, privileged to join in the choice of a ruler, to the level of a mere taxable unit, not only robbed of every vestige of political power, but in many cases metamorphosed into a serf. The Mongol Tatars enslaved the Russians, and the Russians, profiting by the lesson in finance, enslaved their working agriculturists.

So much for the fiscal penalties which the Byzantine policy brought in its wake. Not less heavy were its political burdens. The Slav system differed from all other European methods of government. The right to reign over western nations was based upon conquest; the right to reign over Russia had been conferred by the free choice of the people. The west European state had its foundations in *force majeure;* the old Slav state rested upon the will, freely exercised, of the individuals of whom it was composed. We now see this will ignored with the most cynical disregard for tradition, habit, and equity. In order that one prince may rule over Russia to the exclusion of all the rest,[1] territories like those of Tver, Riazan, Suzdal, and Novgorod-Seversky are wrested from their owners. In order that there may be but one seat of empire in Russia, the great republics of Novgorod, Pskov, and Viatka lose their liberties and go to swell the possessions of

---

[1] Nearly three hundred princes disputed the throne of Kiev alone.

Moscow. At last there is a united Russia. But
there has been no union consented to by the
people. The people have persistently resisted
the centralizing aims of ambitious politicians.
Hence, at whatever shock to the historical
method of dealing with such processes, I must
call the " unification " of Russia a simple usurpation, the "collection of the Russian earth "
by the princes an unvarnished stealing of lands
that did not belong to them. It must be left
to the subsequent events of Russian history to
show what permanent acquiescence there could
be in a policy that, taking advantage of the
national misfortune to effect a mechanical union
of ethnological elements mutually repulsive,
signally reversed the whole course of Slav tradition and history.

The change was one that affected all classes
of society and all forms of the national life.
For autocracy to appear at the apex of the
pyramid without slavery appearing at its base
would have involved a complete negation of
the laws which govern the distribution of social
and political forces. And so one by one come
the dark shadows cast in this eclipse of popular
liberties. First we see the house-servant become
a chattel in the domicile of his master, and
then witness the binding of the toiler in the
furrow to the land which he believes to be his

own. The family, in early Slav times "a republic,"[1] now displays the characteristics of an
autocracy. The father's relation to it is that
of a despot, permitted by the law and enjoined
by the church to keep wives, children, and do-
mestics in subjection by means of the rod.
" Children should be beaten with sticks," says
the "Domostroï," "for the good of their souls."
"The more a child is beaten," wrote Ivan Possoshkov some centuries later, but in much the
same spirit, " the better it becomes." ' " If you
play with a child, you spoil it; the more severely you beat it, the more joy you will have
afterwards." " Love is shown to children in
proportion to the number of beatings given to
them by their parents."[2]

Let us now follow the new despotism into
the domain of law. Here, again, the metamorphosis is complete. Punishments, frightful and
vindictive, have taken the place of the early
humanitarian code. Russia's gaols are chambers
of horrors, red with every refinement and barbarism of cruelty that Mongolism and Byzantinism can together contrive in the interests of
absolute power. Here they are knouting a poor
wretch to death; there, a criminal is being

[1] Karamzin's expression.
[2] The changes wrought in the treatment of women I shall treat
in a special and separate chapter.

broken on the wheel ; in that iron cage yonder,
a " sorcerer " hangs suspended over a slow fire ;
further still, a coiner lies bound with his jaws
forced open waiting for the draught of molten
metal that is to burn out his vitals. Here they
are, digging a hole wherein to bury alive some
woman who, in a fit of despair, has poisoned her
brutal husband ; there, instruments are being
got ready whereby the criminal may be hung,
decapitated, or torn to death piece by piece.

Torture is thus the new method of dealing
with some of the more serious breaches of
Russian law. The penalty of death has been
introduced for homicide ; theft has come to be
an offense punishable by public chastisement.
Not the least signal difference between the
character of the " Russkaya Pravda " (eleventh
century), and that of the " Ulozhenié " (1497)
and the " Sudebnik " (sixteenth century), lay
in the prominence given by the two latter codes
to the remedy of corporal punishment. Under
Scandinavian influence the Slavs had allowed
murder to be regarded as a private injury and
redressed by private reprisal or the payment
of a sum of money. Under Byzantine influence they made all acts of vengeance the business of the state, and for the money penalty
substituted a degrading corporal punishment.
The debtor who persistently continued to be

poor was treated with revolting cruelty. He was subjected to a public chastisement known as the *pravezh*, and ran the risk of becoming the slave of his creditor.

The debtor, it should be remembered, represented crime in one of the most heinous shapes which, in the new order of things, it could possibly assume. The novelties of centralization and autocratic power rested as an immense burden upon the tax-paying classes, and for a man to be found unable to contribute his share of the expenses, or pleading poverty with a view of escaping exaction, must have seemed to Moscow legislators so remarkable a case of human perversity as to call for as severe and ingenious a method of punishment as they could devise.

The debasement of the individual was inevitable. In place of the old manly self-consciousness we find a servility painful to witness, even at this distance. Distinctions of class have appeared, bringing with them practices of self-humiliation and abasement. The noble is as servile to his prince or tsar as is the *muzhik* to the land-owner. In signing their names people write them with unworthy diminutives, in the Eastern fashion. No longer with form erect and look unabashed does the Russian Slav approach his ruler, but in fear and trembling. The very word used for petition means " a prostration," a beating of the head on the ground.[1] It is highly probable that the expression *vinovat* ("I am guilty," corresponding to the English "I beg pardon ") came into existence during this period of universal debasement. Instead of a character like Ilya, the national epic now brings forth Ivanushka Durachok,[2] a hero in caricature, who evades dangers to save his skin, plays the fool in order the more effectually to impose upon people, and attains to honors and dignities by acts of base cunning and low servility. In Ivanushka Durachok we see the new period just as truly as in Ilya we saw the old.

Lying and cunning are first mentioned as Russian vices after the Mongol domination. And if to-day certain classes of Russian peasants, engaged in urban industries, still resort to deceit and subterfuge in compassing their ends, they do so as a result of the straits in which their ancestors were placed by Russian princes and Tatar khans. Cunning in the subject was the natural result of cupidity in the ruler. The more the people came to be regarded as the legitimate prey of the tax-gatherer, the more they learned the force of ruse, the advantage of stratagem, in their struggle with the common enemy. And if deceit arose in this way out of

---

[1] "Chelobityé." [2] "Ivan, the Little Fool."

an unscrupulous system of money-raising, the habit of lying, as it first appears in Russian history, had a not less prolific cause in the national and individual enslavement. The tricky trader, found to-day the victim of corrupting urban influences, is the natural descendant of the class which had to hold its own against the tax-gatherer, or oppose duplicity to the power of the tyrannical owner of serfs. The generous-minded peasant, full of patriarchal simplicity, alike incapable of dishonesty and untruthfulness, belongs in his rural isolation to an ancestry which had not yet felt the Mongol domination, or had passed through it proof against its corruption and debasement.

The main weight of the exactions of grand prince, khan, and tsar must have been felt by Moscow, which, first the nucleus of the coming state, finally became the seat of the new government. And it is of the inhabitants of Moscow that Herberstein wrote, just after Russia had rid herself of the Tatars, "They are more cunning and deceitful than all others." The same people are alluded to in the passage concerning Plescov.[1] "The citizens," says Herberstein, "were dispersed, and Muscovites sent in to replace them. Hence it followed that, in place of the more refined and consequently

---

[1] Probably Pskov.

more kindly manners of the people, were introduced those of the Muscovites, which are more debased in almost everything. There was always so much integrity, candor, and simplicity in the dealings of the Plescovians that they dispensed with all superfluity of words for the purpose of entrapping a buyer."

Such, then, are a few of the ways in which Mongolism and Byzantine Christianity left their mark upon Russian development. The influence of the former was, as we have seen, wholly injurious. That of Christianity was in some respects bad, in others good. To Europeanize the family, as M. Rambaud has described the operation, was an achievement of no small magnitude and importance. But the benefits conferred by Christianity were simply the benefits of a religious system that proved itself superior, for the purposes of civilization, to the faith of the early Slavs. The defects of that system were, on the other hand, the defects of the Byzantinism in which it was naturally entangled. Russia drew much strength and sustenance, much power of patient endurance, during the Mongol domination, from the teachings and ministrations of her new faith; yet her spiritual help in that trying time would have been just as great, might even have been greater, had she obtained it through the Western, instead of from the Eastern Church. The civilization promoted by the Catholic Church was a higher and more promising one than any that could be brought to Russia by the priests of the Greek rite. At the time of Russia's conversion, the civilization of Constantinople was very much inferior to that of western Europe. If Russia escaped Catholicism, she did it by preferring an inferior to a superior degree of enlightenment. If by separating her church history from that of the Poles the country escaped the tyranny of Papal edicts, she on the other hand submitted to a connection of church with state that finally became an instrument as well as a bulwark of absolute power. If Christianity brought refining influences into Russian life, it also imported views and conceptions quite opposed to the martial element of the Slav character; in this way it may have prepared the country to some extent for the Tatar domination. Certain it is that the new faith inculcated greater respect for life — especially for Christian life.[1] It helped to soften manners and to modify in the individual and the nation some of the qualities essential to the successful practice of war. It must be remembered, moreover, that the conversion of

[1] Vladímir, in a direction to his son, wrote, "Put to death no one, be he innocent or guilty. Nothing is more sacred than the soul of a Christian."

the Russians to Christianity was a forcible and not a voluntary proceeding. To this, rather than to the fact that the new faith was thrust upon them by a dissolute prince like Vladímir, are due the long survival of pagan customs in Russia, and the necessity under which the church found itself of compromising with the beliefs which it could not uproot. Nor is this all. In the Slav correlation of forces, all violent reversal of ethnological habits, all negations of racial tendency and tradition invariably reappear in the form of protest. The protest against this forcible indoctrination of the Russians into Byzantine Christianity took the form of the *raskol* or "split," and later came to be known as Russian sectarianism, heresy, dissent.

THERE is no figure, perhaps, in all Russian history upon which the eye rests with greater sympathy and interest than, collectively speaking, that of the Slav woman as we see it, first freely moving in a pagan environment, then subjected to the regulating influences of Byzantine Christianity, and finally emancipated by the teachings of Western culture. It is this figure which seems ever bringing into Russian life, however sad or gloomy that life may be, priceless consolations, impulses of hope and faith and aspiration, as with the odor of flowers and the exhilaration of song. So thoroughly responsive, moreover, has been the position of Russian women to the national vicissitudes that we may fitly divide its story into the same three great periods as those selected for the wider theme. The only difficulty of the parallel is encountered at the outset. As the first coincides to some extent with the polygamous epoch of Russian history, it may seem optimistic to look for much veneration of women in a family of which the conceptions were elementary and the ties loose; yet it should be remembered that, as in most Oriental countries where the institution of polygamy expresses a general permission, but by no means a general practice, the keeping of many wives would be confined to the wealthy classes, and quite foreign to the habits of the poor amongst the Slavs. The treatment of the Russian woman in the pagan period is no more to be gauged by the prevalence of polygamous habits than the civilization of the United States is to be judged by a reference to the practices of Mormons in Utah. Just as the first period of Russian history was favorable to individual liberties, to personal rights, so it was favorable to the status of women. The Slav woman was not less a member of the old family republic than the man; of her influence in it, whether as the spouse of the common peasant, or the confidant and counselor of the earliest Russian princes, there are ample proofs. This Slav woman — polygamy or no polygamy — was quite able to take care of herself and watch over her own interests. In the old chronicles she stands before us strong of will, with plenty of character and patriotism, bold in conception, fertile of resource, capable of lofty heroism and sublime negation of self.

Flames form the setting of the picture that

represents her first noticeable appearance on the stage of Slav history. Numberless Russian women, not yet emancipated from the close attachments of paganism, flung themselves upon the pyres that were consuming the bodies of husbands whom they refused to survive. Euphrasia, whose husband suffered death rather than deliver her to Bati, the Tatar invader, no sooner learned her spouse's fate than she seized her son and with him sprang headlong from the window of her *terem*. When Vladimir, who Christianized Russia, had sent Vassilissa's husband to certain death in battle in order that he might possess the warrior's bereaved and helpless widow, Vassilissa, like a true Slav woman, hurried to the spot where her lord had fallen, and there mingled her own blood with his. In the annals of Novgorod we read how Marfa, widow of the *possadnik* Boretsky, won undying fame as the last defender of Novgorod liberties. Placing herself at the head of the anti-Muscovite party she brought all her energy, boldness, force of character, and wealth to the task of erecting a last barrier against the tide of enslavement that was gradually but surely overwhelming the country; and so successful was the effort that for a brief interval we see Novgorod sheltered from the Muscovite attack by the protecting wing of Poland.

There are abundant evidences that Russian women not only shared in the advantages conferred by that conception of individual rights which, as we have seen, was common to early Slav society, but were specially honored in various ways, notably in their capacity to inherit, and their opportunities of accumulating wealth. Some of the oldest Russian *kurgany*, or burial mounds, have yielded in excavation skeletons of women richly ornamented with jewels. Lybed, the sister of the founder of Kiev, was able to divide an inheritance with her brothers. At the sacking of towns by the Tatars we read of " women, the wives of *boyards*, who had never known work, who but a short time before had been clothed in rich garments, adorned with jewels and cloths of gold, and surrounded with slaves, now themselves reduced to be the slaves of the barbarians." This deferential treatment of Slav women continued up to the eleventh and twelfth century. And as if to carry it to its highest point alliances were sought with foreign princes and princesses. Thus Vladimir Monomakh, himself the son of a Greek princess, took as his first wife the daughter of Harold, who met his death at Hastings. Vladimir's son married a Swedish princess ; one of his daughters wedded the king of Poland, another was united to the king of Hungary. Perhaps the most striking

8

of all proofs of the honor in which the female
sex was held in the first period of Slav history
is afforded by the admission of a woman to the
dignities and responsibilities of government.
The elevation of Olga to the throne of the
princes was one of the last expressions of the
freedom of the early period. And as the complete exclusion of women from participation in
Russian sovereignty through nearly eight centuries characterizes and corresponds with the
political humiliations and social debasements of
the second period, so will the third period be
found one in which, while the nation at large
reaps the benefits of Western culture, Russian
women in one station of life shake off domestic
tyranny, and in another obtain admission to the
highest position in the state.

For the cause of this suppression of women
for nearly eight centuries we must look to the
same set of influences as those which weakened
the free traits of the individual and national
life. Of the two, Byzantine ecclesiasticism was
by far the more important in its influence, and
the more disastrous in its effects. Scarcely have
the priests of the Greek Church begun their
teaching of the new faith to a not over-willing
people when changes begin to unsettle the position of woman, and burden her relationship to
the family and community with a sense of in-

feriority. First, we see her confined to a particular part of the domicile, secluded in the
terem, — an apartment unknown to the early
Slavs, — ostensibly to keep her out of danger and
properly employed, but really to give validity
to the new conception of her subordination to
the master, or despot, of the household. When
the freedom of the tribe, the commune, and the
individual had disappeared, what particular or
plausible argument could the wife offer in defense of her own meagre liberties? If the new
state was to be governed autocratically, what
could be more justifiable than to rest the rule of
the household upon the same foundation? If
absolutism was right in the state, what could
make it wrong in the family? And so, her
status falling, *pari passu*, with the natural extension of the ecclesiastical policy, the Russian
woman at last became the slave of her Christian
husband; as much his chattel as if, under an
earlier *régime*, she had been purchased at mar-
ket or captured in war. The polygamous union
seems to have been one of a voluntary character,
terminable at pleasure. The monogamous marriage was so ingeniously contrived as to be at
once odious by fullness of despotism and indis-
soluble by force of ceremony. The husband
could release himself from its bond by killing
his wife; the wife could become free only by

succumbing to the brutalities of her husband. Whether or not the priests saw in the Slav woman of this period something hostile to the unified state with its monarch an autocrat, thus viewing her with a suspicion which modern rather than old Russian history would seem to justify, — the fact remains that, in marking out for her a position full of humiliating restrictions, the Greek Church was really furnishing to posterity a striking testimony to her influence in the family and in society.

Elaborate measures were taken to counteract that influence. Scarcely had she emerged from swaddling-clothes before her conduct became an object of ecclesiastical solicitude. Boys and girls of the most tender age were not allowed to play together. The didactic writer Possoshkov enjoins the father who happens to witness any playful conduct on the part of his son towards a girl to take a cudgel and break the lad's ribs with it. All social intercourse between young men and young women was forbidden. Even to look at a woman was a sin. Indeed, according to the teachings of the church, woman was not made to be looked at. The priests treated her as a mysterious subject, full of evil potencies, safety from which could only be secured by constant watchfulness. Hence both church and state favored the policy of

seclusion. On the one hand, the *terem* was contrived for the reception of this dangerous element; on the other, the church offered it accommodation in the cloister.

Comparatively few came under monastic discipline, and gave their lives to prayer, discipline, charity. But the mass of Russian women
clung to the duties and debasements of secular
existence with a heroism which is beyond
praise. What they gained from ecclesiasticism
as children we have already seen. As wives,
their sole business was to respond to the caprices of their husbands, to keep house, and
look after food and clothing and servants. They
were to bear children, but not to educate them.
Wives were expected to remain at home and to
know nothing save their household work. Kostomarov, writing of social life in the sixteenth
and seventeenth centuries, says that " women
were generally regarded as being of a lower
order of beings than men, and in certain respects even unclean, since they were not allowed to kill animals for the table, it being
supposed that, were they to do so, the meat
would be unpalatable. On certain days a
woman believed herself to be unworthy to eat
in company. . . . Having become a wife (in accordance with the arrangements of the parents),
she never dared to go from home without the

permission of her husband ; even for her to at-
tend church his consent had to be obtained.
Many women believed they were only born to
be beaten, and that marital love was best expressed with the lash.   Men often killed their
wives, and went unpunished merely because
the death was slow instead of sudden.   When
women poisoned their husbands, as in some
rare cases they did, the culprits were buried
in the ground up to the shoulders, and left to
starve." [1]

The "Domostroï" lays stress on the salutary
effects of wife - beating.   It talks of the lash
much as a doctor discusses doses of medicine.
If the fault is great, the punishment must be
proportionately severe.   If the peccant wife
shows no sign of repentance, she must be lashed
still more vigorously.   The husband is instructed
to hold his victim by the hands, — as much to
render her helpless as to facilitate the beating.
And yet, like the Spanish inquisitor, the husband must be a model of equable temper.
There must be no anger, says Priest Sylvester,
in the chastisement.   The use of wooden or
iron instruments was prohibited, nor were blows
to be given in the face, or about the region of
the heart, in order that blindness might be
avoided and bones be kept intact !!   Thus a

[1] *Ocherk,* etc.   Kostomarov.

Russian husband might torture his wife to the verge of death, provided he did nothing to visibly incapacitate her for the discharge of her household duties. More appalling still is the reflection that this domestic brutality was not only licensed, but actually enjoined by the church as a religious duty. Somewhere, M. Renan has written that Christianity was the religion of women, — that is, a religion created by their ideals, supported by their moral qualities; while Islamism he described as a religion of men. What strength could be expected to flow from the approval of Russian women to a faith which handed them over to cold-blooded outrage and debasement; which bade them bring forth children to tyrants, in order, as in the Buddhist story, that their torments might be repeated in an endless succession of re-births? It is quite true that many Russian women were devoted adherents of the Greek Church; quite probable that, in some cases, the more a woman suffered from Byzantinism, the more faithfully orthodox did she become. But it is equally true that many women who were beaten by their husbands continued to love their tormentors, notwithstanding; and at any rate probable — even if it were not established by the old annals — that the more some wives were thrashed, the better they liked the authors of their chas-

tisement. Love is a mysterious thing, and may
bear a heavy burden of cruelty without breaking down ; and so a religion does not fail of
devotees merely because the way along which it
has come happens to be moist with blood, or
strewn with bones.

Without the good-will of her husband, the
wife was in a position very similar to that of a
political offender who, in Russia, at the present
day, finds himself without a passsport. If delivered for a few brief moments from the *terem*,
— of which, by the way, her husband kept the
key, — she was expected to carry abroad the
humble demeanor exacted from her at home.
If asked a question relating to other than household subjects, it was her duty to reply that she
" did not know." This might be a lie, but she
was bound to obey her husband and the " Domostroï." To the former it was her business
to carry everything heard by her out of doors.
She was forbidden to drink anything stronger
than *kvass*,[1] had no power of making bargains
with peddlers, and was required to have work in
her hand continually. After marriage it was
considered dishonoring for a woman to show her
hair, even to her relatives. The plait, or *volos-
nik*, the sign of virginity, now disappeared in
another form of *coiffure*. In Novgorod it was

---

[1] A non-intoxicating herb drink.

the custom for women to cut off their flowing
tresses as a preliminary to the state of wedlock.
How distasteful it must have been to the Greek
Church for a woman to insist on being attractive after as well as before marriage can be
easily imagined.

A reasonable presumption is that marital beatings diminished in number and severity as a
woman passed from the lower to the higher
walks of life. Seclusion, on the other hand, increased in closeness with rank. Upon the Tsaritsa and Tsarevna the strictest watch was maintained. The princesses were kept in rooms as
far as possible from any thoroughfare. It was
said by a foreign ambassador, writing from
Moscow in 1663, that out of a thousand court-
iers, hardly one could boast that he had seen
the Tsaritsa, or any of the daughters or sisters
of the Tsar. It was even dangerous for any
one to see these high personages accidentally.
The story is told, for example, how Dashkov
and Buturlin, turning a corner suddenly in one
of the palace courts, met the carriage of the
Tsaritsa Natalia as the empress was on her way
to prayers. Although the *rencontre* was purely
accidental, the two were arrested and detained
in custody for several days until the affair had
been "cleared up." Reutenfels states that
when Natalia Krilovna ventured on one occasion

to open the little window of her carriage, the departure from established rules of propriety created a great sensation. Even physicians came under the operation of these rules, since pulses had to be felt and other analogous tactual processes gone through with the face of the royal patient hidden by a veil, and her cutaneous membrane protected from the vulgar touch by a thin gauze!

Herberstein, German ambassador to the court of Vassily Ivanovich, writes naturally enough that "love between those who are married is for the most part lukewarm, especially among the nobles, because they marry girls they have never seen before, and having engaged in the service of princes they are compelled to desert them. . . . The condition of the women is most miserable, for they consider no woman virtuous unless she live shut up at home and be so closely guarded that she go out nowhere. They give a woman little credit for modesty, if she be seen by strangers or people out-of-doors. Shut up at home the women do nothing but spin and sew, and have literally no authority or influence in the house. Whatever is strangled by the hands of a woman, whether it be a fowl or any other kind of animal, they abominate as unclean. The wives, however, of the poorer classes, do the household work and cook, but if

their husbands and manservants are away, they
stand at the door holding the fowl and ask men
who pass to kill it for them.   They are very
seldom admitted into the churches, and still less
frequently to friendly meetings, unless they be
very old and free from suspicion.   But on certain holidays men allow their wives and daughters, as a special gratification, to meet in a very
pleasant meadow." . . .

So much for the women of Moscow and the
remarkable condescension of their husbands.
The general effect of such a policy as that described was to reduce women to a state of the
most abject and helpless ignorance.   Kotoshchin,
mentioning that it was not the custom to teach
them anything in secular branches of knowledge,
speaks of their general incapacity to read and
write, and describes their manners as shy and
awkward, owing to their seclusion and the habit
of permitting them to see only their relatives.
It was probably because of these superficial appearances — the natural results of a treatment
at once absurd and outrageous — that women
came to be so mercilessly dealt with in the proverbial philosophy of the people.   Hence such
sayings as, " A woman's hair is long, but her
understanding is short;" " The wisdom of the
woman is like the wildness of the animals;"
" That which the devil cannot do woman can

do;" "As a horse by the bridle, so a woman must be directed by menaces;" "A bad woman at home is worse than a devil in the wood;" "It is better to irritate a dog than a woman;" "Compared with a quarrelsome woman, the devil is a saint." In a didactic composition of the seventeenth century woman is described as " vanity itself;" "a storm in the house;" "a flood that swallows everything;" "a continually flying arrow;" "a serpent nursed in the bosom;" "a spear penetrating the heart," etc. Another writer of the same period warns men to "fly from the beauty of woman as Noah saved himself from the flood, or Lot escaped from Sodom and Gomorrah," adding that "as Eve did wrong, so the whole race of women became sinful, and the cause of all evil." It is worth while noting that the word for "to marry" in Russian — *zhenit*[1] — means, in a figurative sense, "to deceive " or "cause loss."

How Russian marriages could be expected to turn out happily in the monastic period is a mystery. They were entirely arranged by the parents, the wedded couple being excluded from all intercourse and acquaintance with each other before the ceremony. Nor was the wife always prepared for the household functions within which the church restricted her activity.

[1] Said of the husband, that is, *ducere* as opposed to *nubere*.

"Many girls," wrote the Servian Krishanich, at his place of banishment in Tobolsk, "marry so young that they do not know what a housewife ought to understand. And many of the mothers of these girls also understand nothing of domestic work." So impressed was Krishanich with these feminine defects that he proposed the foundation of schools, wherein women should be taught spinning, weaving, sewing, washing, the salting of fish, brewing, baking, and the making of drinks, adding the suggestion that, before being allowed to marry, each young woman should produce a certificate of her competency in the various branches of household work.

In 1693 the patriarch Adrian issued an order admonishing parents not to marry children against their will. This document marks the relaxing hold of monasticism upon the family, and forms one of the signs of those western influences which were soon to usher in the third and modern period of Russian history. What the reaction was from the domestic tyranny I have endeavored to sketch; how far it gave free play to the intellectual and social forces which had been suppressed during so many centuries; and whether the recoil was slow and healthy or quick and dangerous in the proportion of its suddenness, — these questions must be left for answer to succeeding chapters.

THE RELIGIOUS PROTEST.

THAT sooner or later the people should protest against a system which debased the individual in order to elevate the autocrat, that made land-owners proprietors of serfs, turned princes into tax-gatherers, and gave to every domicile a tyrant and a slave, — this was inevitable. But that the first protest of the kind should have come at a comparatively early period in Russian history, — a period nearly two centuries before the epoch at which the intellectual self-consciousness of the educated classes in Russia can be said to have been fully awakened, — this was partly due to certain special circumstances of the national life. Glancing back for a moment in the line along which our survey has extended, we shall see that Russian development has been a double process, involving singular analogies and contradictions; since, while the state idea has seen its highest expression in the struggle for unity, the masses have found their interest in keeping alive the movement of extension. Migratory habits, enterprise, the natural temptations of fertile land and an open country, — all these stimulated the colonization of European Russia. But to these inducements we must add the element of coercion. The exactions of the tax-gatherer, the numberless tyrannies of the new state, drove the Russian afield into territories where he hoped to breathe more freely. And while this expanding movement did not perceptibly hinder the process of national unification, it sharpened the Slav intellect for coming struggles with absolute power.

The reflective effects of colonization are well marked and beyond dispute. The process is the same, the results are the same, whether the colonizers are from a young stock or go forth to their work from a civilization settled and old. Whenever bodies of men, crossing country or sea, enter a new environment, — a territory in which new varieties of food, new air, water, climate, and scenery are encountered, — and there settle down to the development of social forms and institutions, to the creation of a civilization in harmony with the surroundings, the differentiation of the human beings who engage in the work from the stock out of which they sprang is inevitable. The changes that follow are still more marked when the process of colonization exacts from the colonizer circumspection, boldness, enterprise, activity, and the power of enduring hardships and fatigue. Where these qualities are called forth, the pioneer grows realistic in his views of life and in the conceptions by which his actions are regulated. The sentimental and religious tendencies may still remain; may even be stimulated, by contact with natural forces, into a hypersensuous condition; but the mind as a whole assumes that condition which is usually called "practical." The luxurious wastes and ornaments of old civilizations are discarded and not missed; men learn to conserve their energies and put forth just the amount of force needed and no more. The colonizer becomes a political economist and a thinker; idle habits disappear; spare time is utilized; hours formerly spent in hobbies now slip away in inventions. The immediate interest or necessity is uppermost in all minds. To all actions, planned or completed, men apply the *cui bono* test. Discussion is brief, speech laconic, the deed following the decision with especial swiftness. The new conditions of colonization also give a particular impulse to the development of individuality. Relieved from the crystallized forms of the older civilization, free from the tyranny of its standards and precedents, not controlled, as one inevitably feels in cities like London or Paris, by the spirit of their criticisms, by the utterances of their teachers, by their arts and sciences, their literature, their religion, or their antiquity, — the colonizers begin life afresh in their own way, unshackled, unrestricted, themselves the precedents of the new society which is to arise out of their labors. With everything as yet vague and in the formative state, with a field of operations before it probably vast, individuality sees its opportunity and steps forward. In religion, new churches spring into existence ; in philosophy, should utilitarianism not exclude it, schools arise. The man of ability is immediately surrounded by followers; the man of remarkable gifts carries off the rewards of genius itself. Society, in fine, is led by individuals rather than by coteries, by ideas rather than by maxims, by originality rather than by authority, and by reasons rather than by rules.

It was changes analagous to these — like them in kind, if not in degree — that colonization brought to the hardy and adventurous bands of Slavs who, pushing out from nuclei like Kiev and Novgorod, gradually spread all over European Russia, and were not even kept back by the Ural range, but surmounting it ceased not to advance until the rule of the Tsars extended in an unbroken line from the Baltic Sea to the Pacific Ocean. The work done, the difficulties surmounted in this movement were of an es-

9

pecially trying and arduous kind. Rivers had to be traversed, forests cut down, wild places made habitable. Not always could the pioneers give each other help, such was the insignificant relation their numbers bore to the vastness of the country. And as on the one hand they were exposed to the severities of a rigorous climate, so on the other they had to face the Mongol or Finnish foe, ever on the alert to notice their coming and retard their advance. The rough and ready work of this new life was an education in itself. It taught them self-reliance. It quickened their intellectual activities. It raised them out of a fatalism that was ready to accept everything simply because it was, into an incredulity that questioned on principle and would not be put off with replies that were mere plausibilities. It quickened the sentiment of individuality, and developed anew the old spirit of resistance to usurpations of power, to suppressions of the popular liberties, to negations of private right and personal worth, whether carried out in the interests of state politics, undertaken on behalf of religion, or perpetrated to secure the ends of a coalition at once priestly and regal and disastrous.

And when this first silent protest ripened the Greek Church seemed peculiarly open to its assaults. That institution expressed a double

authority. The source of those great fundamental changes which had banished popular
government from Russia, it became the sup-
porter, not only of its own edicts, but also of
the exactions of the civil power. The Tatars
were among the first to recognize its utility as
an instrument of state, and their politic compromise with it, falsely dubbed "tolerance," formed
no unimportant part of the legacy which fell to
Russia from the Mongol domination. Year by
year the union drew closer, until at last the tension between the awakened realism of the people and the encroachments of the civil power
grew into open and serious rupture.

The real meaning of the outbreak was as
completely hidden from the people who took
part in it as its significance has been veiled
from posterity by the historians. It began in
a trivial and childish controversy. About five
centuries after Russia's conversion to Christianity, errors began to be discovered in the
ritual and service books of the church. These
had arisen in several ways : partly owing to
the practice of copying texts with the pen,
partly to the blunders of inefficient copyists,
partly to the ignorance and incompetence of
the priests themselves. And as the variations
went on multiplying until it might almost have
been said that there were no two Bibles or mass

books alike in all Russia, the Tsar Vassily Ivanovich felt himself constrained to cause a collation of the various texts with the originals, and ordered Maximus, a learned monk of the famous monastery of Mount Athos, to proceed with the work. But the proposed revision was to meet with a vigorous and determined opposition. A powerful party took sides against Maximus, and an ecclesiastical court, *rege volente*, banished the learned monk to a convent. The reform agitation went on. In 1617, the Tsar Michael Fiodorovich had the texts collated anew. Again arose the storm, and Dionysius, the learned archimandrite who had undertaken to succeed Maximus, was sent to expiate his revising zeal in prison. At last the powerful patriarch Nikon threw himself into the breach. With the sanction of the Tsar Alexis Michailovich, the work was now prosecuted with unexampled energy and determination. Nikon secured the coöperation of the œcumenical patriarchs of the Greek Church and the monks of Mount Athos. No fewer than seven hundred ancient manuscripts were brought to Russia in order to facilitate the correction of the faulty texts. In 1655 the patriarch of Antioch, the Servian patriarch, and the metropolitan of Moldavia entered Russia, to offer their assistance. Finally Nikon completed his task,

THE RELIGIOUS PROTEST.   133

and by a great ecclesiastical council, gathered
at Moscow, all who refused to abide by the result were solemnly excommunicated.   At last
the reformers had triumphed.   But the victory
was won in the teeth of an opposition so powerful and widespread that it presented the character of a national movement rather than of a
mere party of resistance within or without the
church.   It was gained under such humiliating
conditions of compromise that while the Russian ecclesiastics eagerly accepted the reforms,
they deemed it politic to throw the reformer
into prison.   Nothing could better illustrate the
imminence of a grave public danger than this
very decision which, while it affirmed the excellence and necessity of Nikon's work, dubbed
Nikon a criminal for carrying it to successful
completion.   Nor could anything better show
the deeprooted and determined character of the
popular protest than the *raskol*, the dissent
and heresy which sprang from the anathema of
the 13th of May, 1667.

The details of the controversy have puerile
and ridiculous elements in almost equal proportion.   The whole question turned on whether
in crossing one's-self the index and middle
finger, or the three fingers, of the right hand
should be used ; whether the word Jesus should
be spelled " Iissus " or " Issus," or whether in a

certain service " Hallelujah " should be sung twice or three times. But does any reader of mine suppose for one moment that out of such absurd elements as these, representing the two extremes of triviality and absurdity combined, a movement could arise fateful for all the subsequent course of Russian history, as serious for the fortunes of the Greek Church as if half its followers had wandered away in some great hegira, and scarcely less grave for social and political solidarity in Russia than would have been the disruption of the planet itself? The issues were not trivial. They were tremendous. Just as beneath the light play of human fancy and the fleeting reign of passion nature conceals some of the mightiest of her processes, so below this petty squabble over the spelling of a name and the raising of a finger lay hidden the elements of a vast convulsion. The reforms of Nikon, the ecclesiasts who sought to enforce them, the Greek Church that forged the anathema; all these represented the state and its complex authority. The Old Believers at first, afterwards the dissenters and heretics, represented the people. The outbreak had long been preparing. A cumulative irritation, a popular spirit of resistance growing deeper and wider with every augmentation of state supremacy, at last enabled the most trivial of con-

troversies to array the rival forces against each
other.

The struggle against the reforms of Nikon
was a protest against authority in both church
and state. This is shown all through the history of the *raskol*. The Old Believers, while
strenuously taking their stand in defense of
points of ritual, showed all through the dispute
a more or less vague consciousness of the political character of the struggle. In declaring the
Tsar to be Antichrist, and declining to pray for
him, they aimed a blow at what was rapidly
becoming the final source of authority in the
double domain of religion and politics. They
made many attempts to provoke the civil power
into reprisals. At Solovetsky, a monastery
built on an island in the White Sea, the protest assumed the character of an insurrection.
Converted by Old Believers banished for their
obstinate championship of the popular cause,
the Solovetsky monks took sides against authority and armed themselves for resistance.
Three years after the anathema had been pronounced, we see the Tsar's troops laying siege
to this centre of disaffection in the far north.
The defenders reply to the attack with a hundred pieces of cannon, and for a period incredi-
bly long, during which the leadership of the
beleaguering forces has to be twice changed,

maintain a sturdy, determined and effective resistance. That at last Solovetsky fell to treachery in no way dims the glory of its defenders. And the brave monks earned a far too terrible reward for posterity to do them the injustice of supposing that for seven long years they held out against the imperial forces simply in order to be able to shout " Hallelujah " twice instead of thrice in a church service, or cross themselves with two fingers instead of three.

· That the spirit of revolt was abroad is shown by contemporaneous events standing apart in their origin from the merely religious controversy. Scarcely a year had elapsed since the excommunication of the Old Believers when a frightful insurrection, the first of its kind, broke out in the governments of the Volga. The serfs revolted against their masters, Cossacks joined each other in armed protest against the curtailment of the privileges, while here and there Tatar, Chud, Mordv, and Cheremiss rose against the Russian domination. At the head of these elements of insurrection Stenka Rázin, the famous brigand, swept the country for three years. At first sight the bond of connection between the two movements seems a wholly general one. But when Stenka Rázin falls into ·the hands of the government, we see a large body of Cossacks, probably the main *débris* of the insurrection, traverse the whole of northern Russia by forced marches, and hasten to reinforce the defenders of the Solovetsky monastery. By one writer we are told concerning this movement that "between the fanatical monks and the Cossacks there could scarcely be any closer point of contact than that they all crossed themselves with two fingers and said Issus instead of Iissus." The probabilities, as well as the facts, are all opposed to so superficial a theory. The point of contact was wider, not closer. The insurrection on the Volga, the insurrection at Solovetsky, were parts of a general revolt against authority, of which the religious controversy and the practice of brigandage formed merely the outward shapes. The inextinguishable energy of the revolt, its superiority to all persecutions and sentences, the endurance of its martyrs, and the glory cast upon their memory by admiring disciples, all bring the struggle into the category of Russian political movements. Reading of the priest Avakum lying for punishment in an underground dungeon in the sixty-eighth degree of latitude, suffering all hardships undismayed, and retaining inviolate his undying faith in himself and his cause, one naturally reverts to modern instances of political expiation;

and when, perusing the story to the end, we see the prisoner not only carrying on a propaganda in chains, but converting his guards to the very views for which it is their duty to hold him captive, receiving confidential communications, holding interviews with agents, and sending men on secret missions with errands which he is powerless to do himself, — all this reads like a page from the contemporary annals of political offense in Russia.

The character of the revolt is further shown by the behavior of the *stryeltsy*,[1] a sort of national militia stationed at Moscow, who were strongly impregnated with the views of the Old Believers. In the reign of Sophia this body, led by Prince Khovansky, broke into open insurrection. The movement was suppressed with great severity, but no punishment could destroy the spirit out of which it had arisen. Again and again the *stryeltsy* rose against the combined tyranny of church and state, again and again they suffered the frightful vengeance of the government, until at last, in a fashion characteristically bloody and barbarous, they were completely extirpated by Peter. The *stryeltsy* were crushed, but not the revolt. It went on widening and deepening in its hold upon the awakening national consciousness.

---

[1] Literally "archers."

Once more it was destined to appear in the shape of armed insurrection. When the Cossack Pugachev rose in 1770 as Peter III., it was upon the dissenters, and still more upon the spirit of dissent, that he depended for success. Pugachev fell like his predecessor, Stenka Rázin, but the protest against authority did not disappear. From " old " belief the movement grew to dissent and heresy, sects sprang out of sects and multiplied to such an extent that, to-day, upwards of 14,000,000 Russian subjects of the Tsar live outside the Greek Church in a state of protest against its authority.

Evidences of this protest the various beliefs of dissent yield in abundance. The Bezpopovtsy, or " priestless " sect, rejects all ecclesiastical authority, bestowing upon its members the right to baptize and perform other priestly functions. So far does this class of dissenters carry its rejection of the older dogmas that it brands marriages within the pale of the Orthodox Church as illegal. The Philippovtsy[1] are notorious for their fanatical hostility to the state. The Fedoseyevtsy[1] reject the orthodox sacraments and the institution of the priesthood. The Stranniki (Wanderers) regard as an essential part of their doctrine the suspension of all relations with the church and state.

[1] From names of persons.

The Duchobortsy (Warriors of the Spirit) teach the negation of all dogmas. Under Catherine II. and Paul I. their attitude was one of pronounced hostility to the state. The Strigolniki [1] direct a vigorous polemic against the church. The Molokani decline to acknowledge Orthodox sources of authority. The members of a sect known as the Nyemolyaki (Prayerless People) imitate the Vosdykhantsy (Sighers) in their opposition to Biblical authority and all forms of religious supplication. In this sect, as in the Molchalniki (Silent) who reject the Bible, and disbelieve in a future life, in God, and in religion, we see the negation of authority carried to its utmost possible extreme. One body of dissenters selected the Russian passport system as the object of its special hostility. The Stundists, at the beginning of their existence as a sect, expressly disavowed their presumptive subjection to the state.

A sort of atavism is noticeable in not a few of the sectarian articles of faith. We see the dissenters falling back, unconsciously· enough, to the dogmas — religious, social, and political — of the early Slav life. · The Obshcheyĕ, (Commune) taught a purely communistic doctrine. Every *mir* that joined it was forthwith

[1] From a proper name.

erected into a communistical unity, the members of which enjoyed all property in common under the administrative direction of " twelve apostles " regularly chosen from the people. The Stundists believe in and inculcate the equality of all men, exacting from members of the sect a pronounced fraternal and philanthropic activity. Regarding commerce for profit as sinful, they trade with each other by a process of simple exchange. Land, water, and cattle they regard as the property of all men in common, and as incapable of being transferred in inheritance. The popular character of early Slav legislation finds an echo in the Stundists' practice of settling all disputes amongst members *inter se*, sometimes with the aid of an elder temporarily invested with judicial functions. In the principles of the Duchobortsy, who hold that all men are equal, and that children ought to have the same consideration and reverence paid to them as that shown to adults and the aged, we catch a glimpse of old Slav life, with its recognition of personal worth and individual rights. This sect disbelieves in a future life, asserting the *post-mortem* migration of the soul either into another body, or to some far-off planet, — a partial reversion to the old Slav dogma that after death the soul sometimes journeyed to sun or moon. In the case of not a few of the fanatical sects, a truly pagan scorn of marriage has wrought not a little injury to morals; at times some of the heretical dissenters link themselves in their atavism with the erotic orgies of the ancient world.

The motive force of the revolt called dissent was Russian individuality. We find it everywhere awake. Men ready to lead, groups eager to be led, are ubiquitous. The *raskol*, with its one "split," gives birth to a thousand. A new idea in dissent, a shade more of faith or incredulity in any given direction, the discovery of some affirming or denying text in the New Testament, that armory of arguments for sectarians, —any one of these causes was amply sufficient to start a new creed. The influence of individuality in sect-forming is shown by the large proportion of dissenting systems of faith that bear the names of their founders. Thus, from the activity of Daniel Vikulin the Danielites came into existence; that of Theodosius Vassiliev led to the organization of the Theodosians. In the former sect an extraordinary influence seems to have been exerted by a certain Prince Andrei Dennisov Myshetsky, who left behind him a voluminous literature on religious subjects. The same passionate enthusiasm and restless activity in the cause were displayed by Simeon, his brother and successor. The founder of the Philippovtsy, one Philipp, caused himself, with thirty-eight of his followers, to be burnt alive. A case is also narrated in which seventeen hundred sectarians set fire to their village and voluntarily perished in the flames, denouncing the Church, the Tsar, and the Orthodox priesthood. In the commune of Starodub, government of Vladimir, one Daniel Philippovich gained such influence over his followers that they consented to receive a series of " ten commandments " at his hands. The peasant Kondrati Selivanov, regarded by his Khlysty followers as the incarnation of God, but at last whipped by the authorities and exiled to Siberia, there became the centre of interest for hundreds of pilgrims who visited the leader in his banishment. Over the spot where Selivanov suffered the punishment of the lash they built a chapel ; out of the materials of his life they composed a legend of passion and martyrdom not unlike those of which, more recently, Russian political patriots have been made the subject. Gabriel Simin, the Cossack founder of the Nyemolyaki ; Kapustin, leader of the Duchobortsy ; the venerable Abrossim, chief of the Zhivniy Pokoiniki ; Michael Ratuzhny, who originated the Stundist movement ; these, and many others whose names might be given, were all men of awakened self-consciousness and powerful individuality. Nor did women escape this intellectual re-birth. At times their enthusiasm ran over into fanaticism. The Skoptsy (Self-Mutilators) had amongst their members in Morshausk, government of Tambov, a peasant woman named Anna Safonovna, who was held in great veneration as a prophetess. Amongst the Khlysty (Self-Whippers) numerous "mothers of God" and prophetesses have made their appearance. The absurdities into which the enthusiasm of the time led the softer sex are further shown by the career of women like Akulina Ivanovna, who led a thousand followers as the ": Queen of Heaven," and of Anna Romanovna, who wielded influence by such means as ecstasies, paroxysms, and prophecies.

WESTERN ENLIGHTENMENT.

THUS far it has been the strange and abnormal lot of Russia to take her institutions from the foreigner, aud to have by no means the most excellent of them foisted upon her against her will. We have seen how she first called in the Varegs to teach her government and military organization ; how her next appeal was to the Greek Church to instruct her in ritual and religion ; and how, from numerous foreign sources and at various times, she drew laws, customs, industries, and arts. It is now for us to look upon Russia under foreign tutelage in what may be called the European or modern period of the national life. This nominally begins with the reforms of Peter; really, its advent antedates that monarch's birth by several decades. It is to Poland, the vulnerable side of the empire, that one naturally looks for the advanced-guards of the new civilization. The Poles were already an enlightened race and had a literature, long before Russia had yet produced her first writer of note. Under Alexis Mi-

chailovich, in the seventeenth century, the habit
had sprung up of employing Polish teachers in
the wealthier Russian families.   In high places,
too, this same Polish influence made itself felt.
Western manners obtained a footing at the
courts of the Tsars.   Helen Glinsky, the second
wife of the Tsar Vassily, and mother of Ivan the
Terrible, persuaded her husband to shave his
beard nearly two centuries before Peter's forcible introduction of the practice.   The influence
of Marina in promoting western culture at the
court of Demetrius, her husband, was still more
marked.   But when we come to the reign of
Peter's predecessor, Russian receptivity for
European civilization seems to enter upon a
new stage.   Alexis, the father of the reformer,
showed in himself that love for foreign institutions which he transmitted to his son.   A traveler to some extent, he had frequent intercourse
with foreigners, and in the house of Matveiev
met the most cultured men and women of the
time.   Polish and Little Russian influence was
strong during the reign of Alexis ; and of the
immigrant savants, teachers, and theologians
who wielded that influence, some were chosen
to teach the children of the Tsar.   Stronger
still, perhaps, as a Europeanizing force, was
the German colony at Moscow, representing the
best enlightenment of the time, as a. sort of

entrepôt through which a select few were permitted to draw otherwise contraband stores of culture and idea from the countries of western Europe. It was in the German colony, moreover, that the regulations of the "Domostroï" were first broken through in regard to woman, who there took her proper place in society.

The new influences proved fatal to domestic tyranny. Tanner writes in 1678 that men had begun to permit their wives to converse with other men in their presence ! What it cost the priests to be obliged to sanction this arrangement is nowhere stated. A little later, Korb reports that "women no more hide themselves, but go to church in open wagons." A new period is clearly at hand for the long-oppressed slave of the Russian household. In 1677 and 1679 legislation is enacted in favor of property-holding by wives. Woman, after eight centuries of exclusion from the Russian throne, again takes her place at the head of the state in the person of the regent Sophia,[1] who in intellect, enterprise, force of character, and education, fitly represents the awakened feminine consciousness and aspiration of her time. The ad-

---

[1] To be followed, in due course, as Empresses, by Catherine I., the two Annes, Elizabeth Petrovna, and Catherine II., — a whole galaxy of feminine talent.

vent of Peter brought, if not the complete
emancipation of women, a host of reforms in
their favor. The *terem* was abolished. Henceforth Russian women were to appear in society
and dress in the European manner. Parents
were prohibited by law from causing children
to marry against their will, while the betrothal
was legally fixed to take place six weeks before
the marriage, in order that the couple might
become acquainted with each other, and break
off the engagement if they thought necessary.
The law forbidding uneducated gentlemen to
marry was an attempt to bring enlightenment
into families which stood in far greater need of
culture than of wealth. Servile diminutives
and prostrations were no longer permitted; to
wear his beard and continue to be a Russian
Slav entailed upon each subject who refused to
shave a fine of from thirty to one hundred rou-
bles; the *pravezh* took a milder form. Numerous foreigners were brought to Russia; many
books were translated into the language of the
country, to the end that its institutions and industries, its manners and customs, might thence-
forth belong to European rather than Russian
civilization. So sudden and violent were the
reforms that even church literature underwent
their modifying influence. The orthodox youth
is warned by Possoshkov that he must not pay

court to two or three young women at the same time, on the ground that " woman is not an animal, but a human being." The same writer counsels husbands to undertake nothing without first advising with their wives, remarking, " She is, before God, not his servant, but his helper. She is not even a mere helper, but equal with the husband. Even when the wife is intellectually incapable, you must hear her counsel, if only to carry out the will of God. If she gives bad advice, God will help the husband to see what it is necessary for him to do."

Peter originated no new movement, but merely gave a sudden and violent impulse to a process already begun. He incarnated the spirit of the time. All its tendencies found expression in himself. A genuine migrant, he had an intense love of travel. His predilection for the foreign amounted to a passion ; his eager receptivity for knowledge linked him with the people. That he was the most realistic Russian of his time — perhaps that Russia has ever produced — is shown by the practical character and studied utility of all his reforms. Like those of the people, his aspirations were upward and onward, for racial movements carry monarchs along with them as well as slaves. Yet despite these common points of agreement to facilitate understanding with each other, it was

inevitable that hostilities should break out between a ruler who lived in the future and subjects whose predilections lay in the past. Peter
was a Slav like the rest, but unlike the rest he
was born an autocrat, and could no more rid himself of the influence of circumstance than could
the classes over whom he ruled. The people
could not brook absolute power, and Peter could
not brook popular power. Traditions which,
under one set of circumstances, produced popular
hatred of monocracy, under another set arrayed
the individual against pantocracy. It was the
union of two passions, one individual, arising
out of position, the other racial, a product of
growth, that gave so much harshness to the reformer's character and activity. Had Peter
been less of a Slav he would have been less of a
despot. On the other hand, had he not been
born to power he might have won it for himself. His struggle against the popular resistance had especial elements of difficulty. He
had ascended the throne in the full tide of a
thinly disguised political revolt. By all the
methods which it could compass — by church
secessions, by religious insurrection, by brigandage and risings — the country had expressed
its resistance to authority. Peter not only con-
ceded nothing to that resistance : he provoked
it with every expedient of a fertile brain, and

then foiled it at the top of its bent by bringing against it all the instruments of brute force which an unlimited command of the resources of punitive cruelty placed at his disposal. It was the same old issue that Peter now revived with a thousand aggravations. Just as merely superficial appearances failed to explain the quarrel between Nikon and the Old Believers, so there was a deeper meaning in the new dispute than any that could be drawn from the outer aspects of a petty squabble between the advocates of Slav institutions and the partisans of west European civilization. In the one as in the other case the popular revolt was against authority and all that it represented; against centralization, against beaurocracy, against undue tax-gathering; against, in fine, the combined burdens of an ecclesiastically and autocratically governed state.

Jealous of every authority save that of the Tsar, Peter took early steps to secure the field of sovereignty wholly to himself. To the popular resistance he opposed the inquisitions and barbarities of a secret tribunal. The privileges of the Little Russians he struck down by abolishing their hetmanate. By a series of terrible massacres he broke the power of the *stryeltsy*. Distrustful of the monks, whose sympathies were not with the reforms, he forbade them the

use of pens and ink in their cells.   He warned
the bishops against display and ostentation, in-
structing them to receive and permit no marks
of popular reverence.   The dissenters were re-
lentlessly persecuted.   Peter could brook no
rival, even in spiritual matters, and so, abolishing the patriarchate, he became as supremely
head of the church as he had been before in-
contestably autocrat of the state.   Finally, we
see him — distrustful even in the paternal relationship — sanctioning the murder of his own
son.[1]

Peter's egoism and energy, his ambition, his
callous insensibility to human suffering, seemed
to give autocratic rule in Russia a new and vi-
rile lease of power.   The Tsar reformer left the
Russian state superficially stronger than ever,
— stronger by its union with the church, by
pressure of the nobility into its service, by a
more perfect system of money-raising, and an
increase in the authority of the proprietorial tax-
gatherer over the enslaved tiller of the soil directly related to the increased authority of the
monarch himself.   But Peter did more than
simply perfect this half Mongol, half Byzantine
legacy that had fallen into his hands.   The existing system was essentially Asian.   Peter
sought to make it European.   Previous Tsars

---

[1] Knouted to death.

had been content to build up the Russian state
homogeneously; Peter and his reforms raised a
problem that was destined at last to form the
one great question of the national life, before
which all others were to be of mere secondary
interest. How long and to what degree was it
possible to reconcile to the old *cadre* of autocratic government this filling in of western culture? How many centuries could Tsarism hope
to go on pouring out the bright new wine of
modern civilization into those ancient bottles of
Asian despotism that Europe has never tolerated save in her curiosity shops? In the light
of questions like these Peter's work possesses a
double significance. Constructively, and within
the immediate limits of his activity, the reformer did more to strengthen the foundations
of despotism in Russia, perhaps, than any other
member of the Romanov family. Unconsciously
and prospectively, he struck despotism a blow
from which it was destined never to recover.
No avowed champion of the people, aided by the
most favorable circumstances, could have done
such effective battle for Russian liberties as that
compassed by the champion of absolute power.
Earlier than the reforms by a century had the
West sent out into the Russian land her pioneers of enlightenment; like the serpent brood
at the root of Yggdrasil, the world-tree of Scan-

dinavian myth, they lay gnawing at the base of autocratic rule, silently, if slowly, undermining that structure of ages to its fall. But Peter was the first to fairly robe Russian tyranny in the Nessus-shirt of European civilization. This was the reformer's real significance for the national life. This was his title to greatness and to glory.

Eagerly welcoming as enlightenment what it had resisted as authority, Russia, once fairly in the new path, went on steadily assimilating west European manners. The courts of empresses and emperors became brilliant centres of foreign culture. Under Anna Ivanovna German influence reigned almost as despotically as the Tsaritsa herself. It was the privilege of Elizabeth Petrovna, who opened relations with France, surrounding herself with French emigrants, to witness not only the first successes of the new civilization, but also the birth of Russian literature in Lomonossov. Foreign influence, principally French, fired the wit as it embellished the reign of Catherine II., and only culminated, under Alexander I., in a brilliant epoch wherein Russia seemed to follow the example of France by crowding the most illustrious of her names into a single page of the national history. In some of the earliest years of the century now about to close, we see Russia not only saturated with the science and learning of the West, but mature enough to have a national literature of her own.   From Kantimir, Derzhavin, Karamzin, Zhukovsky, representing the foreign and unripe period of the new culture, the country grew to Pushkin, Gogol, Koltsov, Krylov, Griboyedov, Turgeniev, and others, representing the national or introspective period of the intellectual movement. The emancipation of the serfs, the impulse given to popular and university education, the spread of the literary spirit by reviews and newspapers, all events of the reign of Alexander II., seemed to bring Russian civilization to its highest point.

What, now, was the character of this progress?   Did it tend to reconcile the people to authority, or was its influence one provocative of hostility to the system of rule by absolute power?   It must be remembered that then as now the Russian government, alike in the manner of its origin and the methods of its operation, was a unique national phenomenon in Europe.   It was in the autocratic order of society that all Russian literature, uninfluenced from without, had its foundation.   The foreign literature read so eagerly by the receptive Russians presupposed an entirely different constitution of society and order of things.   When least political in its character it offered numberless contrasts with Russian life; when most political it formed a literature of propaganda. Enlightenment, even when pure and simple, was the foe of all despotism; knowledge used to glorify liberty could not fail to hasten the processes that were disintegrating a semi-Asian state. Such had been the influence of the foreign culture and ideas that in the first years of the century we see Alexander I. consulting with statesmen whose ideal constitution was a government in the English and not in the Russian manner. Montesquieu, Rousseau, Byron, Goethe, Schiller, had an audience in Russia fully as eager and impressionable, if not as large, as that to which they appealed amongst their own countrymen. Griboyedov, in "Goré ot uma" (The Misfortune of having Brains), and Gogol, in "The Revisor," supplied the material for gloomy comparisons of Russian with west European civilization. In the third and fourth decades of the century we see the Russian youth studying Schelling and Hegel, absorbing the doctrines of Fourrier and St. Simon. The art school of Bielinsky finds its antithesis in the realistic school of Pissarev. Popular translations of the works of Darwin, Büchner, Moleschott, and Buckle are eagerly read. The students devour Prudhon and Louis Blanc. Chernishevsky in the sixth decade popularizes the writings of

John Stuart Mill, and formulates, in "Shto dyelat." (What 's to be done), a scheme for the reconstruction of society. The socialistic ideas of the time find expression in the "Contemporary," in which both Chernishevsky and Dobrolyubov champion western thought.

Such, briefly, was the European period of Russian development. That it was a period of high and valuable acquisition for the national life is incontestable. The machinery of the first reforms was unquestionably despotic. Foreign manners were frequently associated with foreign morals. But a real and beneficial enlightenment took place. Western culture, in emancipating women and children from domestic tyranny, merely anticipated by a few years an inevitable reaction from the sway of the "Domostroï." Foreign literature stimulated native minds until the Russians could create a literature of their own. It was foreign ideas that led to the emancipation of the serf; it was foreign ideas that gave the country imperfect yet priceless educational advantages; it was foreign ideas to which must be referred all concessions of absolute power to absolute subjection that have been made in Russia during the present century.

On the other hand, we have seen how intolerance of autocracy increased in proportion to

the degree and character of the incoming enlightenment. The greater the Russian's love
of foreign institutions, the greater was his de-
testation of those at his own door. Science
gave an immense impulse to this critical intro-
spection. The realism that produced incredulity in matters of religious faith led to the rejection of the most venerable dogmas in politics.
If now and then "emancipated" circles of
young people deemed it proper to reject authority in the family, and withdraw reverence from
the sacred mysteries of the church, what obe-
dience and consideration could they be expected
to show to the head of the state? The very
sanctity of life itself came to be questioned.
What was nature, reasoned the young material-
ist, but an eternal process of reproduction and
annihilation, a process in which life is continually purchased at the cost of death, a process in
which the general and not the individual weal
is the supreme law? If by the death of one
man millions could be made happier, would not
that be a gain? Such was the terrible questioning that arose out of the new knowledge from
the West, and such the exaggerated forms in
which the issues of a great problem had begun
to present themselves. Yet they were nothing
more than a natural reaction from the evils of
a system which the Russian mind was rejecting

with a dangerous suddenness, rather than in a movement of recoil at once slow and safe. The emancipation of women could not fail to present phenomena of an analogous character. Of Russian women in 1843 Haxthausen writes : —

"If, instead of going into Egypt to look for the free woman, the Saint Simonians had made a voyage to Russia, they would have come back perhaps more satisfied. In a family well organized, it is the husband who reigns and the wife who governs; but in Russia it is quite the contrary. Many of the peasant women work very much less than with us in the country districts. Men in Russia even perform part of the household work: they carry water, wood, and make the fire. Amongst the *bourgeoisie* and merchant class the women pass the day doing nothing."

And when, in comparatively recent times, young female students donned male garments and cut their hair short like that of men, the vagary was not nearly so unnatural as it seemed to the many superficial observers who held it up to ridicule. The reaction was from a state of things for which hardly any exaggeration could furnish an adequate antithesis. No peculiarity of attire or manner could so unsex woman as she was unsexed by the *terem* and the " Domostroï." The wonder is not that she rebelled, but that she did not rebel in some more terrible and tragic manner.

FIRST FRUITS.

IF the state policy of Peter was faithfully continued by his successors, the spirit of revolt was kept alive by the miserable condition of the people, and by the numerous provocations they suffered at the hands of autocratic power. Scarcely had Catherine II. ascended the throne when a terrible insurrection broke out in Moscow. The mob cried, "It is not for us Orthodox to suffer the injustice of authority!" Two years later an extensive rebellion was led by Pugachev, who gathered under his banner fugitive serfs, dissenters, Volga pirates, and men of all reputable and disreputable classes from the Volga regions. The rising was in itself of small significance. "It is not Pugachev that is important," wrote Catherine's agent; "it is the general discontent." The serfs rebelled against their masters; the Tatar tribes rose against the Russians; a frightful revolution seemed on the point of shaking the empire to its fall. But Tsarism acted promptly; Catherine hung Pugachev and destroyed the Zaporog republic of free Cossacks. A few years later the *dilettante* empress amused her favorite nobles by making them presents of human beings, a step which transferred one hundred and fifty thousand men and women from the crown lands, where their lot was tolerable, to the conditions of private serfdom, where it was incomparably more wretched. In 1767 the correspondent of Voltaire issued an *ukaz* forbidding serfs to make complaints about their masters and mistresses, .and giving to the latter the right to deport the slaves to Siberia. Later, Catherine established serfage in Little Russia.[1]

It was in the reign of Catherine that the revolt against authority, hitherto expressed in general discontent or in outbreaks that aimed only indirectly against the existing *régime*, began to take the form of conspiracy. At first the movement seems to have sheltered itself in freemasonry societies, and to have been confined to the planning of an improved form of government for Russia, such as might be discussed amongst the intelligent classes without exciting suspicion. Its leader in Catherine's time was one Novikov, who did much to disseminate the new culture amongst the masses, who afterwards suffered from the disrepute into which

[1] Was not this the lady of whom Voltaire wrote, "C'est du Nord, aujourd'hui, que nous vient la lumière"?

freemasonry fell, and finally came to be regarded by some as the father of the Russian
revolt. But the modern and aggressive phase
of the revolt had not yet begun. It took the
cumulative irritations of three reigns after that
of Catherine to give it anything like a permanent footing in Russia. Of these, the schemes
of Paul for the support of sovereign authority
were amongst the first signs of the distrust with
which the successors of Peter began to regard
European ideas. At first Tsarism had deluded
itself into the belief that it could combine a
state organization as despotic as that of Russia
and a civilization as advanced as that of England or France. Gradually, by force of mere
suspicion at the outset, afterwards by the logic
of facts, this simple faith gave way to a recognition of the utter impossibility of holding together a dual state, of which the ruling elements
were irreconcilable with each other. To lessen
the antagonism, to correct the harm already
done, Tsarism hit upon the expedient of filter-
ing foreign ideas through the censure; in urgent
cases, of excluding them altogether. A panic
fear of the West and of Western influences displayed itself in many of the measures of Paul
and his successors. In close attendance upon
it we seem to see in the autocratic mind a vague
consciousness of injustice, a sense even as of guilt

that could not be shaken off. This overwhelming disproportion in the balance of power on the
side of the ruler, the crowding of all final authority into a single individuality, the practical
annihilation of the people as factors of national
government, — all these pressed upon the representative of Tsarism with crushing weight.

Alexander I. began by coquetting with Western culture, and ended by holding it in profound
distrust. He had a particular fear of the foreign pedagogue and governess.

"Our nobles," runs a state paper of which Alexander approved, "the support of the empire, are
brought up frequently in the care of persons who . . .
despise everything native, and have neither sound
acquirements nor proper moral principles. The other
classes imitate the nobility, and help to compass the
overthrow of society by handing their children over
to foreigners to be educated. . . . Foreigners are also
chosen to impart instruction in the sciences ; this
doubles the injury, and is rapidly rooting out the
national spirit."

In order to remedy the state of things com-
plained of, Alexander decreed that in future the
founders of private schools should be tested for
"morality" rather than for knowledge. An
ukaz issued in 1824 enjoined the closest watchfulness upon the censure, in order that influences might be counteracted that were spreading

" immorality, infidelity, and sedition." An *ukaz* of the same period aimed at suppressing the school circulation of certain " dangerous " works. From the universities several professors were dismissed. The further teaching of natural philosophy and the political sciences was forbidden. The students were henceforth required to live in the fear of God and the Orthodox faith, to show the due respect and hold themselves in proper subordination to all officials of the university and the state, to refrain from attending theatres and social gatherings without permission, not to go beyond the limits of the town, even on botanizing tours, without the authority of the school chief; not to be seen in public taverns or hotels, not to read books inimical to the Orthodox faith or to the existing method of government, not to leave the university or school without permission. The press was crippled and a ban laid upon the teachings of Newton and Copernicus. The earth still moved, but not for Alexander; the apple continued to fall, but the Russian monarch had made up his mind to ignore the phenomenon. Such were some of the irritations contrived for the towns and town life. Alexander also found time to guard the agricultural populations against evil influences. In a number of districts he established military colonies. The scheme was one for recruiting the army without crippling agriculture, and for keeping up a healthy sentiment of loyalty amongst the common people. These ends were to be accomplished by the unmarried soldiers of each colony becoming the husbands of the peasants' daughters. The wretched *muzhik*, upon whom the whole weight of the state lay, resented this new burden. In the new temper of the people, his revolt against authority took the direct form. It was repressed with great cruelty.

Unfortunately for the success of Alexander's plotting against Western ideas, there was one inlet for them which no rigors of censorship could close up or even hold in surveillance. The Napoleonic wars and the part Alexander played in them had brought some of the most thoughtful men and officers of the Russian army into direct contact with west European civilization. No longer mere students of the French revolution, drinking in from books the teachings of the Encyclopædists, at last they stood in Paris, in the heart of that bright world of ideas, upon which they had gazed so ardently and so long from the dark planet of their own destiny ; at last thousands of observing Russians, belonging to all ranks in the army and militia, seemed to have broken through the restrictions upon foreign travel, and to be wan-

dering over western Europe, comparing their
own lot with that of the foreigner, storing up
impressions and experiences, collecting knowledge, and committing facts to memory, that
were afterwards to cross the frontier in too in-
tangible a shape to suffer interference at the
hands of censor or officer of the custom house,
yet full of a potency that could not be esti-
mated in terms of physical force. The true
and first propaganda of the revolt began when
these traveling Russians carried back to their
countrymen at home the story of what they had
seen in Europe. Many of them, like Pestel,
noticed that " the states in which no revolution
had taken place continued to be deprived of
many rights and privileges; " not a few of the
officers recrossed the frontier with the fixed
purpose of "importing France into Russia."
In 1815 the two brothers Muraviev founded the
" Arsamass," a literary society with political
objects. At first the conspirators hoped to obtain a new constitution by peaceful agitation.
But the "crowned Hamlet" of Russian autocracy, as Herzen called him, blighted these
hopes by closing all the Freemasons' lodges,
and by harassing the more enlightened classes
through the censure and the police. In 1817
the " Alliance du Bien Être " came into existence under the leadership of Pestel. Then

followed the Society of the North, with its headquarters at St. Petersburg, and the Society of the South, stationed at Moscow. The Society of Virtue was dissolved, but two other organizations stepped into its place. Over the four societies now in existence Pestel's influence was predominant. The general object of the conspirators was to set up a federated Slav republic or constitutional monarchy. Pestel planned the seizure and execution of the royal family, and the proclamation of a new government by the Senate and the Holy Synod, who· were to be forced into the part assigned to them by a military insurrection. Many soldiers were gained over to the scheme, but the outbreak itself was badly carried out, and had no leaders worthy of the name. Prince Trubetskoy, the head elect of the new government, was nowhere to be found in the moment of danger. When at last the outbreak came Alexander was dead, and Nicholas, with an insurrection barring his way to the throne, plied the two thousand revolting soldiers with grape shot. The rising was easily crushed. Pestel, Ryliev, Sergius Muravev, Bestyuzhev-Ryumin, and Kakhovsky expiated their aspirations and bravery on the scaffold; one hundred and sixteen others were banished to Siberia.

This first conversion of the spirit of revolt

into terms of force ended in an apparent disaster for the conspirators. Yet it was the conspirators who were really victorious. Nothing could have given so vital and stimulating an impulse to the cause of Russian revolt as a failure which was destined to array the very worst tendencies of absolutism against the rising intelligence of the people. Nicholas was a born despot, but his despotism as a Tsar drew not a little of its selfish egoism and unbounded cruelty from the irritating events of the 14th of December. Had .the purpose of the Dekabrists been to show autocracy at its worst, and in this way to array against it all the potencies of popular resistance, their success could not have been greater than it was. Had Nicholas aimed at calling forth all the bitterness and hostility which the hearts of his subjects could cherish towards despotic rule, he could not have acted more in harmony with such a purpose than he did. A monarch so ingenious in devising methods of popular irritation perhaps never sat on the Russian throne. We see him laying his iron hand on everything that could be suspected of contributing to the fast growing discontent. Foreign travel, the study of foreign languages and literatures, teaching by foreigners or by Russians who had been educated abroad, — all these were made the subject of numerous prohibitory or restrictive decrees. The inculcation of German philosophy he ingeniously confined to the priests, the majority of whom did not know the language of their own liturgies, not to say anything of the tongue of Schelling and Hegel and Kant.

The revolt gradually obtained recognition in official circles. Attempts were even made to explain it. Numerous rescripts and decrees, particularly school orders and university papers, declare the harm to have arisen through the idleness of the student, the " luxury of half knowledge " wrought by the prevailing system of education, and the immoral influences of private tuition under the care of foreign masters and pedagogues. The elements of the problem awaiting solution are thus summed up by Uvarov, minister of public instruction, in a report to the Tsar dated 19th November, 1833 :—

" Russia has preserved a warm faith in certain religious, moral, and political ideas peculiar to its own conditions and circumstances. But how shall these principles, which lack unity and centrality, and have had to sustain an uninterrupted struggle during the past thirty years, be brought into harmony with the present temper of the times? Shall we be able so to include them in our system of universal education as to combine the advantages of our own time with the traditions of the past and hopes for the future? How may we devise a system of popular education which shall correspond with our own state of things and yet not be foreign to the European spirit? Whose strong and experienced hand can keep intellectual aspirations within the limits of quiet and order, and at the same time ward off everything likely to prove inimical to the welfare of the state?"

Or, in other words, "How shall we reconcile a European culture with an Asian method of government?" It was the old issue. Uvarov was seeking a *modus vivendi* between the two forces, and he was clearly aiming at the impossible. Western ideas had already shown their hostility to Tsarism, and no experiments with education, no dismissing of professors, no crusade against foreign teachers, foreign books, and foreign travel could force the new thought into a degrading compromise with its highest verities and aspirations. The revolt was to awaken again, and that right quickly. Mr. Wallace tells his readers that there was little need for the order that went forth after the hanging of Pestel and his fellow patriots, — the order declaring "that there should be no more fireworks, no more *dilettante* philosophizing or new aspirations." "Society," says the writer named, "had discovered to its astonishment that these new ideas . . . led in reality to exile and the scaffold. The pleasant dream was at an end." A society that could give birth to men like Pestel, and Ryliev, and Bestyuzhev, — to men who, under happier circumstances, would have been the salvation of their country, — was not a society to underestimate the hazards of a struggle for liberty, or to basely yield up its aspirations because suffering and bloodshed were to be the penalties of realization. The " pleasant dream" was not at an end. It drew a fresh charm from the intensified despotism of which it was the bright antithesis ; it furnished generous minds and hearts with an ever recurring means of escape from the dreary life of the new *régime.* And when at last tyranny at home and dragooning abroad brought Nicholas to the ignominious reverse in the Krim, all tongues that could give voice to the common aspiration for liberty arose in condemnation and arraignment of the absolutist monarch. From one end of the empire to the other this voice was heard, in manuscripts, in pamphlets, in books. The people declared they had been " kept long enough in serfage by the successors of the Tatar Khans." They protested that God had not condemned them forever to be slaves.

In the mean time a movement was spreading in Russia that, hitherto regarded as an outcome of mere literary and ethnological sentiment, must here be restored to its true place and significance as a part of the general revolt. In this, as in many other cases, one cannot fail to recognize the extraordinary vitality of the process which is assailing the fabric of Tsarism. The revolt never dies. Driven from one means of aggressiveness, it selects another point of attack. Its approaches are often as cunningly indirect as those of a besieger's parallel. Whether as a religious quarrel, as an act of collective brigandage, as a military revolution or a conspiracy, it preserves its character and aims through the most baffling and Protean disguises. We shall next see it, then, in association with the protest against that authority which forced upon an unwilling people the innovations of Peter, the reformer. That protest had a double character. In their negative attitude the people resented the inroad made upon their personal liberties, or upon so much of them as remained; their positive opposition arose out of a love of the free life of the early Slav period and its allied sentiment in favor of old Russian habits and customs. Gradually this protest grew into a declared opposition to west European culture, and gradually a class of thinkers was formed who began to decry everything foreign and laud every thing Slav and national. Russia had all the elements for such a reaction within her own borders. The profound distrust with which many educated people regarded the reforms was intensified amongst the people by a natural hatred of the despotism with which they had been enforced, — a despotism which grew as the state grew, and with every extension of imperial authority placed new burdens upon the shoulders of the masses. The war with France, the "patriotic" uprising against Napoleon, the triumphs of Pushkin in the national field of Russian literature, and the introspective direction given to thought by the writings of Gogol, —all these helped to strengthen a movement ostensibly directed against foreign culture, but really aimed at a *régime* which withheld from Russia the advantages of its old civilization.

Under the impulse of literary romanticism on the one hand, and of German philosophy on the other, the movement or tendency at last separated intellectual Russian society into two parties. Both elements, conservative and liberal, we see represented in the third decade of the present century by a group of young men who met to study Hegel at the house of Stankevich, a university professor in Moscow. One of the questions discussed was, " Is a logical transition possible, without gap or obstacle, from pure Being through Nothing to Becoming and Existence?" In other words, " What governs the world, the free creating Will, or the law of necessity?" Further, "In what consists the antithesis between the Russian and west European civilization? Is it the degree of the development, or the peculiarity of the elements of culture?" Finally, "Is Russian civilization destined to be penetrated not only by the superficial results, but also by the fundamental substance of European civilization? Or will Russia, after she has absorbed her own Orthodox intellectual life, find in this a new phase of universal human culture?" A political turn might be given to almost any one of these questions, yet they seem to have been discussed without reference to questions of state. The immediate result of the controversies which sprang from them was the formation of the two parties,—the Slavophils, or Nationalists, and the Zapadniki, or Westerns.

Both were discontented with the existing *régime*. The Westerns, whose polemical headquarters were St. Petersburg, admitted the lack of self-consciousness on the part of society, and the helplessness and ignorance of the masses, but looked for a means of remedy to the dissemination of European knowledge and the consistent prosecution of the work begun by Peter. The Slavophils, who found their party centre at Moscow, had a policy in harmony with their choice of camp. They looked for help to the past, in which they saw, instead of tormenting discord, a full unity between authority, society, and the people. They held that the reforms had separated the masses from the upper layer of society, which had abjured them. Thus the national unity had been destroyed. To restore that unity it was necessary to reject Western culture and return to the old Russian civilization.[1] M. Ivan Aksákov, one of the cleverest and best known of the Slavophils, describes the reforms of Peter as having effected a complete revolution. " The state," he goes on to say, " breaks with the country and subjects it. It hastens to build a new residence that has nothing in common with Russia, and has no root in Russian reminiscences. While it breaks faith with the land, it forms itself on the pattern of the West, where state institutions have been most developed, and introduces the aping of western Europe. Everything Russian is persecuted. Those of the state serve it faithfully; the people remain true to the old. Russia is split into two. It has two capitals. On the one hand is the state, with its foreign capital St. Petersburg; on the other are the people, with their Russian capital Moscow."

The Slavophils carried on no conspiracy against Tsarism and had the happy fortune not

---

[1] In this paragraph I follow the account given by M. Pypin in vol. ii. of the *Vyestnik Yevropy.*

to be suspected of disloyalty.   Yet their views
and policy, — formulated not only by M. Aksakov, but also by talented men like the brothers
Kiryevsky, like Khomyakov, Valuyev, Kon-
stantin, Samarin, Koshelev, Yelagin, Novikov,
Shchiskov, — will be found to raise issues against
Russian absolutism precisely identical in essence
with those of the revolt itself.   From the very
group of Slavophils who had been studying
" non-political " philosophy with Stankevich
sprang two of the most uncompromising foes of
Tsarism that Russia ever produced.[1]

The Slavophils had a clear predilection for the
political characteristics of the old civilization.
They were opposed to the evils that had been
wrought by the usurpations of the autocratic
state.   In dwelling on the unity which the old
Slav system secured for authority, society, and
the people, they were simply lauding the privileges of the pre-Muscovite days, of the time when
the people had their *vechés,* when the ruler was
a servant, when the communal and urban liberties were intact, and when the population governed their own country, *neminem ferans imperantem.*   Nothing had done so much to cause
that separation of classes of which they com-
plained as the growth of the autocratic state
and the gradual sacrifice of healthy social equali-

[1] Herzen and Bakunin.

ties to the financial exigencies of a centralized administration and a unified territory. The error, sentimental rather than historical, into which the Slavophils fell was that of choosing the pre-Muscovite period for idealization, and of blaming Peter alone for a work of class separation which, it is quite clear, began long before the advent of the reformer, having really been originated under Byzantine and Mongolic influence.

When Slavophilism grew into the wider ethnological conception of Panslavism, the movement showed its inner solidarity with the revolt in new forms. The aim of the party was to bring into a union more or less close all the branches of the Slav stock. The scheme further contemplated the headship of the Tsar, and the Russification of the various members of the union. Finally a fraction was born to Panslavism under Koshelev, who withdrew his consent to the Russification of the Poles, and demanded a new constitution for Russia.

A remarkable feature of the Panslavistic sentiment was the federative idea which underlay it. Herzen, for example, planned a separation from Russia of the Caucasus, the Baltic provinces, and Finland. Others contemplated Polish and Little Russian autonomy. The dream of not a few Panslavists was a federation of all the

Slav nationalities.   And this idea of federation directly connected the movement with the revolt, since it was a reversion to the federative principle of old Slav life.   We shall see later how it was utilized and developed by the opponents of the unified empire.

MYSTICISM AND PESSIMISM.

IT now becomes necessary, before the story of the revolt can be resumed, to consider certain psychological phenomena due to the oppressive conditions of the individual and national development. The mystical tendencies of thought in Russia seem to have first declared themselves on religious ground, but their later manifestations have invaded all fields of intellectual life and literary labor. Mysticism, the reader will remember, has worn innumerable garbs and received multifarious definitions. It has been called theopathetic, theosophic, theurgic. It has been discovered in the Vedas, in the doctrines of Plato, and the philosophy of Hegel. In the Middle Ages we see it as "purification," "illumination," "ecstatic union," and "absorption." Sometimes it is pantheistic, sometimes theistic. Strictly speaking, it is an internal illumination, a supersensual exaltation, an ascribing of objective existence to the subjective creations of the mind. But the name has also been given to morbid tendencies to the mysterious, and to the play of the fancy in the realm of the spiritual or ghostly. In the individual the mystical condition may be produced by some striking experience, — by a crushing disappointment, by world-weariness, by the discovery of some truth. It may arise in deep melancholy, still oftener out of despair. Yet, with depression for its exciting cause, it appears only in the form of reaction. The mind seems to triumph over its old state by a sense of exclusiveness and exaltation, a consciousness of special endowment, sanctity, or knowledge. Mysticism, as a national trait, is produced by oppressive conditions of national life; mysticism in religion arises out of dry and lifeless formalism. Yet, in whatever guise it may present itself, mysticism is ever the result of irritation, and always assumes an attitude antithetical to authority, whether the dogmas opposed be theological or political.

Russia is by no means the only country of Europe in which mystical tendencies have given their color to intellectual life and religious movements. Spain had her mystical reaction after the crushing of constitutional and religious freedom by Charles and his son Philip. Germany affords a still more conspicuous example in the mysticism of the "Sturm und Drang" period. A whole nation's longing for liberty, for fullness of knowledge, for the lost simplicity and delights of childhood, were nowhere so well expressed as in " Faust," that most mystical of all Goethe's literary work. By turns, or yielding to a common impulse, other countries than Spain and Germany also had their mystical periods. Yet there is a fundamental difference between the mysticism of Russia and that of western Europe. The former is chronic; the latter acute. This, as we know it in literature, is long ago dead; that was never more vital than it is to-day. West European mysticism may be called a phenomenon; Russian mysticism is essentially a growth.

The first considerable appearance of mysticism in Russia took place simultaneously with the development of dissent from the *raskol.* It was the peculiarity of the mystical sects of the eighteenth century that they found converts exclusively amongst the peasants, and sprang up in parts of the country separated from each other by great distances. Mystical dissent appeared not only in the southern provinces, but in Finland, in the Caucasus, at Moscow, Kaluga, even in Irkutsk and Kamschatka. These facts show —unless intellectual tendencies, like plant seeds, can be scattered by the wind — that Russian mysticism was a purely native growth, having no sort of relation or connection with the Anabaptism or Quakerism of the west. Its most pronounced features seem to have found expression in the Dukhobortsy sect, to which reference has already been made. The great mystic and leader of this body was Kapustin, who, proceeding from illumination to illumination, at last declared himself to be Christ, and was worshiped as such by his followers. Kapustin reasoned in this wise: " Has not Jesus said, ' I shall remain with you till the end of time?' Thus from century to century, descending from generation to generation, the divine soul of Christ has resided in a succession of men in whom, during its temporary sojourn in the imperfect body of a child of man, it has conserved the remembrance and consciousness of its divine extraction. During the first centuries of Christianity this truth was known to all men. At first the man in whom the soul of Christ resided was the Pope, but there came false Popes. Christ has said, ' There shall be many called and few chosen.' " The chosen, according to Kapustin, were the Dukhobortsy.

Such, indeed, was the mental tension out of which dissent arose in Russia that there is scarcely a sect in existence to-day in the dogmas of which mystical leanings are not discernible. The conditions of Russian life in the seventeenth and eighteenth centuries had lain upon

minds and hearts with so heavy a weight that
the people were glad to fly for relief to the wildest dreams, to the strangest faiths, to the most
fantastic illusions which highly wrought religious ingenuity could invent. The Tatar domination was long over, but a new domination
had arisen, more powerful and more relentless,
of wider range, of deeper humiliation. The
more centralized the state became, the heavier
had grown the fiscal burdens of the people ; the
greater the autocracy at the summit of national
life, the greater the enslavement at its base.
Nor was there any sufficing help for this state
of things in the ministrations of the Greek
Church. Minds that found it a source of light
and life during the dark hours of the Mongol
oppression now looked vainly for consolation to
the national faith. Its assumption of authority,
its alliance with the civil power, its Byzantine
elements, all prepared it for the *raskol*. But
it was the dreary, lifeless formalism of its worship that sharpened the dissenter's longing for
a freer and more vital spiritual activity than
any that it could attain within the limits of authority and tradition.

In religious soil Russian mysticism bore abundant fruit, and is active as an element of dissent
to this day. We also see it in the "men of
God" of the political propagandas and conspira-

cies of 1873. But it was destined to occupy a
still wider field. Waiting on the new culture
from Europe it gave its color to some of the
earliest productions of the national literature.
Scarcely a single Russian writer of note is altogether free from the wider tendencies of mysticism ; not a few have manifested the quality in a
degree highly marked. Pushkin had an especial fondness for the weird and spiritual elements
of the national legends. Gogol, with a predilection for the fantastic not less pronounced, became a confirmed mystic in his later years. The
Russian painter, Ivanov, surrendered himself
completely to religious mysticism. Some of the
later works of the novelist Dostoyevsky, notably "The Brothers Karamasov," are mystical
to the point of saturation. That strange story,
"Clara Milich," written by Turgeniev not very
long before his death, is pure mysticism. It
raises a singular issue, and decides it in the
affirmative; that is to say, Can love enter the
living heart and influence the emotional nature
after the object of it has been committed to the
grave ? Another example is afforded by Count
Leo Tolstoï,[1] the author of that much admired
novel, "War and Peace" (Vainá i Mir), who
quite recently, in a fit of religious exaltation,

---

[1] Not to be confounded with the late minister of Public Instruction, Count Dmitri Andreyevich Tolstoī.

pronounced his literary works idle and sinful. Destroying his poems, the Count began the composition of a work on the teachings of Jesus Christ, with a lengthy introduction narrating his own religious experiences. On the completion of the book it was " prohibited " by the Holy Synod, the result being that only a fragment of it has obtained circulation in Russia. The mystical element is strong throughout. The introduction [1] narrates the author's struggles to solve the problem of his own life, his despair and leaning to suicide, his final questioning of religion, and " illumination."

The case of Count Tolstoï, in harmony with all available evidence on the subject, shows that the tendency to mysticism is one which invariably manifests itself late in life, or at any rate grows more pronounced with increasing years. This coincidence of the individual process with the racial and historic process is of itself evidence that neither in the one case nor in the other is the phenomènon any mere accident, but a part of the national life and a result of its conditions.

It is, at the same time, true that a complex mental condition like mysticism can only have a limited field of activity and manifestation. The tendency really universal in Russia is to

---

[1] Printed at length in the *Obshcheyay Dyelo,* No. 57.

pessimism. This penetrates all spheres of thought, gives its hues to every coterie and school, creates resemblances between the most diverse productions of the pen, restores as with a bond of gloom the shattered solidarity of society, and between human beings separated by impassable gulfs of rank and position stretches a connecting link of dreary despondency and common despair. Mysticism enters readily into composition with some elements; with others it is uncompromisingly irreconcilable. Pessimism goes everywhere, combines with everything. Not to be pessimistic in Russia is to be divorced from all contact and sympathy with the national life; to be cut off, either by foreign birth or by some monstrous denial of nature, from the tree of the national development. All influences and epochs have contributed to the tendency. A monotonous landscape, the loss of free institutions, Byzantinism with its cruel law-giving and ascetic tyranny, the fiscal burdens of the new state, the antitheses suggested by European culture, the crushing of the individual, the elimination from Russian life of all those healthy activities which engage citizenship in other countries, the harassing restrictions upon thought and movements, the state-created frivolities of society, — all these have contributed to the gloom of the mental atmosphere until to-day pessimism may be said to be the normal condition of all Russian thought. In religion it produced, as in the Zhivniyé Pokoiniki sect, assertions of the evil of existence and the misfortune of birth. In literature it has given its tone to the finest efforts of the poet and the novelist. The lives of Pushkin, Lermontov, Gogol, Dostoyevsky, and many others of Russia's greatest men were passed in a perpetual struggle with the pessimistic tendency. It was Lermontov who called life a "stupid, empty jest." When Pushkin had read a few pages of Gogol's "Dead Souls" he exclaimed, "My God, how sad our Russia is!" Herzen doubted whether it was possible for any Russian to be genuinely merry. He called the Russian laugh a *ricanement maladif.* Dostoyevsky spoke of ideas themselves being in pain, like patients.[1] And Nekrassov, a true poet of the people, heard everywhere the voice of the national woe : —

> " Where moaneth not the Russian man ?
> In the fields he groans and in the roads, *
> And in the mines, and on the railways;
> He groans in the telega, nightly journeying through the steppe,
> And in his own miserable little cottage."

Or the Volga itself is made conscious of the ubiquitous pessimism : —

> "Volga, O Volga! In spring many-watered!
> What groan ascends from thee, great Russian river?

[1] In *Byedniyé Lyudi* (Poor People).

That groan we call it singing;
There burlaki the hawser pull.
But, Volga, thou dost not the fields so inundate
With thy broad waters as this people's sorrow,
This mighty woe, fills all our Russian land." [1]

" Russian sadness " — *russky pechal*, as Nekrassov called it — invades all the inner life of
the people.   Yet it is singularly unobtrusive in
social spheres.   I know of no altruism more
agreeable than this power which Russians have
of separating themselves from the interests of
their own individuality, in order that they may
contribute gaiety and liveliness to the general
enjoyment, — this cheerful *insouciance* below
which, sacrificed to the social exigencies of the
moment, melancholy, sorrow, all depths of despair may lie hidden.   It is this versatility that
constitutes the chief charm of Russian society.
But the Russian has his inner as well as his
outer world, and between the two stretches
a distance relatively immense.   The outer is
shown to strangers and acquaintances ; with
the inner only íntimates and relatives come
into contact.   Hence the ease with which the
Russian nature is misunderstood, or only inad-
equately comprehended, by foreigners.   Hence,
also, the inevitable failure of all attempts to
explore the Russian mind or the Russian country, with only French or German for one's interpreter.

[1] From *Razmyshleniya u narodnova padyezda.*

Is it not the Russians rather than the English who take their pleasures sadly? Even in the village festivals, the liveliest of all Russian popular out-door enjoyments, there is a lack of earnest merry-making, a want of boisterous joyfulness and *abandon*, almost a shrinking from relaxation and amusement, that leave a painful impression in the mind of the sensitive spectator. I never looked upon one of these festivals without thinking of the women who, as Herberstein tells us, were permitted at certain times of the year, "as a special gratification," to meet each other outside Moscow "in a very pleasant meadow." The prohibitions of the "Domostroï" linger about the gathering; men and women alike seem in doubt whether they have a right, or can afford, to be happy; only the children can be said to enjoy themselves, for they represent the early period of Slav history, the time in which the people were the free arbiters of their own destinies. This half-fatalistic fear of happiness, or, let us say, of the mere phantom of it, somewhat in the spirit of the German lines, —

> "Oh, Freude, habe Acht!
> Sprich leise,
> Dass nicht der Schmerz erwacht!"

is also noticed in the cities. On public holidays, or days of so-called national rejoicing, the crowds which closed factories and places of business dismiss to the streets wear a gloomy and spiritless aspect utterly out of harmony with the idea of out-door enjoyment. On the other hand, rejoicings by *ukaz*, in celebration of events imperial rather than popular in their interest, call forth a most ludicrous half-heartedness on the part of those who participate in them.

A full harvest of pessimism may be gathered by the quiet eye of a stroller through the public gardens of any of the large Russian cities. One of the finest of these resorts is the Lyaytny Sad, or Summer Garden, in St. Petersburg, — a spot of green that in warm weather daily attracts thousands of visitors, and remains full of music and pedestrians until long after midnight. Here the crowd is strangely subdued in its manner. Everybody seems absorbed in his own reflections. Army officer, student, *chinovnik*, governess, all wear the same aspect of serious gravity. Couples pass along without seeming to converse; before the orchestra hundreds sit listening, or promenade through the *allée* amid a silence unrelieved by a solitary laugh. Dress deepens the prevailing gloom, since it is characterized by a striking lack of color, most of the women being attired in black. A cemetery might furnish more convincing proofs of the vanity of life, yet it could scarcely attract a crowd more mournful than that which goes its sad, mechanical rounds on summer nights in the Lyaytny Sad.

There is also a noticeable pessimism in nearly all Russian music of a popular or national character. A strange plaintiveness, increased by frequent resort to the minor key, is heard in countless songs of the people ; the effect is often so peculiar that it is difficult to express it even in notes. The saddest of these melodies are sung by students at their gatherings in the university towns ; the weirdest, perhaps, take the form of recitative and chorus, heard mostly among the peasants and common people of the country districts. And if Russian music is sad, Russian street cries are infinitely sadder. Anything so mournful as these I never heard. Hour after hour, day after day, with the window of my apartment in the Troitsky Pereulok open upon the quadrangle below, have I listened to the voice of the vender. Sometimes it was a youth, but oftener a man or an old woman, and always the impression has been the same. It was a cry, and yet it seemed a song. And such a song ! Heart-piercing it was, and sank into one's soul. It was a 'shriek of pain, an exclamation of anguish, a wail of despair. It had a life independent of the singer. The vender might go with his basket of wares and return no more, but the lamentation was always rising, and remained ever the same. No single human being, however miserable, I used to think, could have composed it ; nor was it the product of any guild, or locality, or even epoch. To me it seemed the rhythmic utterance of centuries of suffering. I saw in it, I heard in it, only the accumulated burden of the people's woe condensed into a single cry of anguish, and that cry committed to the keeping of the wretched and the miserable for all time.

THE DYNAMIC PERIOD.

THE despotism of Nicholas ushered in a new era for the revolt. The movement widened and deepened. From being the affair of a mere coterie, it began to occupy all classes of educated society. It rose to the dignity of parties. It brought the Liberal, the Nihilist, the Socialist, the Revolutionist, the Terrorist, one after another, into the arena. Its newspapers appeared and were circulated through Russia in tens of thousands. It established its *Vehmgericht;* it carried on its propagandas; it compassed against absolutism the most deadly assaults known in the history of political conspiracy. That three decades should have sufficed for the maturing of a movement so terrible in its methods, so inexhaustible in its resources, so indomitable in its spirit, — should, moreover, have witnessed its triumph over all the repressive means which Asian and European civilization could array against it, — shows abundantly that the country was already ripe for the outbreak when Nicholas called it into being.

Individualism opened the new period with a bitter and cynical reaction against the moral and social obligations. It aimed at being a law to itself. It repudiated all dogma and tradition. In the religious domain it championed materialism; to morals it gave a utilitarian basis; social standards it rejected outright. It was a gospel of pure negation in which, while men sought freedom for their individuality, women thronged to the schools and universities in quest of the means of independence. Much has been said to show that at first this nihilistic movement had no political character, and yet all its protests were aimed at the principles and traditions which lay at the foundation of the Russian state. At bottom it was the same revolt against authority as that of the dissenters in the days of Nikon. And from a negation of moral, religious, and philosophical principles it rapidly progressed to the negation of dogmas in politics.

Socialistic doctrines had already gained a footing in Russia when the young adherents of Slavophilism met to discuss philosophy in Moscow. The interest awakened in the writings of Louis Blanc, Proudhon, St. Simon, Owen, and Fourier led in time to the formation of certain associations, the members of which met to discuss passing events and literary productions.

Some of these societies gradually assumed a political character, giving birth to what is known as the Petrashevsky conspiracy; but on the breaking up of that organization in 1848 by the police, most of the associations collapsed.

For a few years longer Nicholas maintained the iron system which is associated with his name, and then it fell, and great was the fall thereof.' The year in which Alexander II. succeeded to the throne brought new champions to the side of the revolt. At home Chernishevsky preached political economy and a guarded form of socialism in the "Sovremennik;" abroad, Herzen, from his printing-press in London, thundered against the vices of Russian absolutism. The new emperor himself posed as a reformer. His address to the people at the close of the Crimean War excited the wildest hopes. A national springtime seemed at hand. The fetters fell from the press. Thought was set free. Everybody hastened to declare himself a Liberal. Such was the fever of the time, such the relief from the nightmare of the previous *régime*, that even immature youths in the educational establishments felt themselves moved to prepare new schemes of reform.[1]

That a reaction of disappointment would follow was inevitable. The reforms which were

[1] Mentioned by Eckardt.

in everybody's head had no place in the schemes
of the emperor himself. It soon became clear
that there would be no radical concession to the
revolt. The authorities even undertook to re-
strict discussion of the changes decided upon.
The marshal of nobles in the government of
Tver was exiled for having permitted a debate
on the subject. Finally came the act of 1861.
The serfs, who had been attached to the glebe
in the interests of the state, were now, alike in
the interests of the state, invested with the
rights of free cultivators, it having been found,
as M. Rambaud justly observes, " that a people
in which the majority of the agricultural classes
was subjected to serfage could not rival the
European nations in intellectual, scientific, or
industrial progress."

But the act of 1861, however desirable, necessary, or inevitable, did not wholly satisfy the
peasants,[1] nor did it, even supplemented by the
judicial and administrative reforms which followed, meet the highest wishes of the country.
It was so far from being a concession to the revolt that its immediate effect was to intensify
the movement against absolutism. The reac-
tionary steps which followed added fuel to the

---

[1] A hundred of the protesting serfs, the reader will remember,
were forcibly emancipated by one of Alexander's officers, General
Apraxin. He shot them.

flames. The government at first confined itself to harassing the student classes by withdrawing from them the right of assembly and association. The outbreaks which followed were repressed with characteristic severity. In the same year a secret society, composed of army officers, issued an address to the emperor demanding for Russia constitutional government, for Poland complete freedom and self-rule. The nobles also began to agitate for a share in political power. In 1862 the authorities closed all the clubs and reading circles known to be in the service of the revolt. Amongst the institutions thus attacked were a large number of Sunday-schools in which the propaganda had been carried on. The "Sovremennik" was suspended, and Chernishevsky[1] thrown into prison.

Thereupon followed the Polish insurrection of 1863. As the smoke of that outbreak cleared away new methods and machinery of aggression were seen to be in possession of the revolt. A number of clubs had sprung up in various parts of the country, ostensibly for educational and philanthropic purposes, but really to facilitate propaganda. Amongst these were the Pensa

[1] "Pardoned" in 1883, and permitted to return to Europe after nineteen years of exile in Siberia. At present in Astrakhan, under close police surveillance, practically a prisoner.

Club, founded in 1861, and the Zemlya i Volya (Land and Liberty) organization, established a year later. Simultaneously with the club movement came a systematic distribution of contraband literature, smuggled across the frontier by Sergei Kovalek and others, amongst artisans in the towns and peasants in the country districts. The personal work of the propaganda was mainly carried on by Ishutin Khudyakov, Prince Cherkesov, Karakasov, Yurassov, and Sagibalov.

For three years the revolt gave no other sign. Then a bolt fell from the blue. On the 4th (16th) of April, 1866, Karakasov, as delegate of one of the clubs, fired at the emperor as the latter was leaving the Summer Garden on the Neva side. The attempt failed. The representative of absolutism owed his life to the promptitude of a peasant. Yet the conspiracy had an immediate and important effect upon the general agitation. It has always been the lot of the revolt to profit by its own excesses, and so the effect of Karakasov's shot was genuinely cumulative. The government entered upon a policy of reaction that not only drove many outsiders into the movement who would otherwise have remained aloof from it, but gave the theoretical nihilism of the time a turn that was to bear serious fruit at no distant date.

An imperial rescript declared order, property, and religion imperiled, — though the real danger was the danger to absolutism, — and Count Tolstoï, called to the Ministry of Public Instruction, at once devised and carried into effect a scheme for harassing the youth of the schools and universities. Three years later the Nechayev conspiracy was organized. Its leading spirit, with the help of funds obtained in Geneva, aimed at a general rising of an anarchical character. For a time the preparations went forward without interference, but on Nechayev using his influence to procure the murder of a conspirator deemed " unsafe," the police broke up the organization, and out of three hundred participators, a number were punished, including Nechayev [1] himself.

The revolt now drifted into a new policy. Of the puerilities of mere negation every one had grown heartily tired. A practical activity was needed, of which the results should be positive and substantial. Hitherto the agitation had been mainly confined to the towns. Gradually the conviction came that the country at large must be invited to take part in the undermining of absolutism. What could a handful of conspirators, however energetic, hope to ac-

[1] Sentenced in 1872 to hard labor in the mines, but said to be still confined in the Alexeyev Ravelin at St. Petersburg.

complish against a principle supported by the
loyalty of fifty millions of peasants? On the
other hand, everything was to be hoped from
the sympathies and participation of the people.
In this way and under the stimulus given to it
by the secret press, now driven abroad, but there
powerfully inspired by Bakunin and Lavrov,
the revolt entered upon its socialistic phase.
Thereupon began a movement which, whether
one regards its character, the aims which inspired it, the forces which it commanded, and
the sacrifices it involved, or the cruel disappointment in which it ended, must be pronounced to have no parallel in history, and to
have been only possible to the Russian country
and the Russian people. No sooner had the
word gone forth that the people were to be
prepared and enlightened for outbreak than
hundreds of volunteers offered themselves for
the work of propaganda. Young people of both
sexes forsook the parental roof, or left their
studies at school and university, to hasten by
every road and highway and river with their
message of enlightenment and revolt to the
country districts. In order to win over the people and make the task of tuition all the easier,
many of these enthusiasts put on peasants'
attire, gave a blowzed appearance to their faces
by rubbing them with grease, or steeped their

hands in brine until they became as rough and hard as those of the *muzhik* himself.

Young men who had been delicately brought up learned the trade of the blacksmith, the carpenter, the shoemaker, or the locksmith, in order to come more immediately into contact with the artisan classes; young women of the best families worked in the factories like common peasants, or took a share as agriculturists in the labors of the field. Sometimes the propagandist would be a tutor in a nobleman's family, or a governess engaged to teach languages in the house of a land-owner, or even a woman doctor, winning friends for the cause in the guise of an *accoucheuse*.

The activity of these apostles of the revolt was twofold. On the one hand, the peasants and artisans were stirred up to discontent by *vivâ voce* statements of the people's wrongs; on the other, they were approached by means of an enormous flying literature of propaganda that took all shapes in which it was likely to appeal to the agricultural and laboring classes. Schools for the propaganda in the guise of workshops were founded in St. Petersburg, where Prince Krapotkin frequently gave lectures to the artisans in socialism. The propaganda possessed similar machinery in Moscow. In the government of Novgorod, Sophie Leschern von Herzfeld, daughter of an army general, started a village school and-there gave instruction to the peasants in the principles of the revolt. A smithy in the government of Tver, kept by the peasant Paul Grigoryev, served as a place of propaganda for a large district. Centres for the movement were also formed by workshops in Yaroslavl and Saratov; by a gun factory in Tambov; schools in Chernigov and Kamenny-Podolsk; a farm in Kovno; and clubs in Pensa, Kasan, Ufa, Orenburg, Nizhni - Novgorod, Kharkov, Yekaterinoslav, Poltava, and Kiev. The agitation was carried into every government west of the Ural range. The propagandists are said to have numbered several thousands in all. Amongst them were Enduarov, the rich proprietor and justice of the peace, of the government of Pensa; the wife of Golushev, chief of gendarmes at Orenburg; Dukhovsky, professor at the Yaroslavl Lyceum; Kotelev, president of the government administration in Vyatka; Portugalov, the writer; Sophie Subbotina, a rich land-owner; Sophie Peróvskaya, daughter of the General Governor of St. Petersburg, and niece of the Minister of Public Instruction.

Some of the propagandists sacrificed their whole fortune to the cause, like Yermolov, who maintained several student comrades until the time was ripe for "going to the people," or like Voinaralsky, a justice of the peace, who spent 40,000 rubles in furthering the agitation. All suffered the greatest hardships. Yet despite the enthusiasm, the self-sacrifice, the energy expended upon it, the movement proved a failure. Success was impossible. The people were not ripe enough for a revolution. The propagandists were not mature or experienced enough to prepare one. With a simple faith even more credulous than that of the peasants whom they hoped to convince, they neglected the commonest precautions, scarcely concealed their movements from the police, in some cases allowed their mission to become matter of public notoriety. The authorities took early action against the propaganda. Hundreds were arrested and thrown into prison. In two years the "pilgrimage to the people" movement of 1872-74 was practically at an end.

The next phase of the agitation was to have a strongly revolutionary character. Tired of preaching doctrines which the peasant found it difficult to understand, but above all disappointed at the smallness of the harvest reaped from so much devotion, the friends of the revolt now applied their energies to the fomenting of outbreaks. A "settled" agitation took the place of the wandering propaganda amongst the people. Agents of the revolt established themselves in small towns, villages, and hamlets, and thence proceeded to excite the population against the authorities. For the purposes of agitation amongst the artisan class, unions and associations, with revolutionary aims, were formed in St. Petersburg, Moscow, Kiev, Odessa, and other centres. (The boldest of all these new propagandists was Jacob Vassilyev Stephanovich, who in 1876 organized a conspiracy in Chigirin, government of Kiev, that had over a thousand participators, embracing the male population of about thirty villages. A day had been fixed for the rising, but the police, informed of the project through the incautiousness of the conspirators themselves, broke up the organization before it could mature its plans, and lodged nine hundred of the peasants concerned in prison. In the spring of 1877 the members of a revolutionary society called the " Narodniki " (Party of the People) " went to the people," establishing a large number of propaganda centres along the line of the Volga.

But the most terrible epoch of the revolt was yet to come. The general hopelessness of the prospect, the cruel severity of the government reprisals, the failure of all milder measures to ameliorate the situation, drove the parties of the revolution to extremes. (In 1878–79 the revolt entered its terroristic period. Already in September, 1876, Gorinovich, the spy, had been shot by Leiba Deutsch in Odessa. In the same month Tavleyev, also a spy, fell the victim of the conspirators whom he had betrayed. Fisogenov, a St. Petersburg spy, was murdered in the following year. Early in 1878 the notorious Vyera Sassulich shot and wounded General Trepov, police prefect of St. Petersburg, for his cruel treatment of a prisoner, the student Bogolyubov. The sixteen-year old heroine of this episode became the object of a universal sympathy. Vyera was acquitted by a jury, and, aided in her escape from " administrative procedure " by a street crowd, reached Switzerland in safety. Early in 1878 four spies were shot : Nikonov in Rostov, Fetissov at Odessa, and in Moscow Rosenzweig and Reinstein. Sembrandsky, of Kiev, who wore a coat of mail, escaped, but afterwards took his own life. In the same year an attempt to take the life of an obnoxious court official named Kotlyarevsky in Kiev resulted in failure. Baron Heyking, chief of the Kiev gendarmerie, fell in the street, stabbed to the heart.

The repressive measures of the government had been growing in severity. The slightest offenses against absolutism were met with the most disproportionate punishments. For an insignificant disturbance in Kiev, one hundred and fifty students were dismissed from the university and thirty banished to a northern province. The courts had grown vindictive and partisan. The law of trial by jury was daily ignored. Prisoners acquitted by the ordinary processes were systematically brought under administrative procedure and banished or imprisoned afresh without trial. The spy and denunciation system had become intolerable. The crusade against the revolt was carried on by a secret and unscrupulous organization of police, known as the Third Section. Prison life was unendurable. Revolts broke out in the Fortress of Peter and Paul at St. Petersburg and in the central prison at Kharkov. So badly were the prisoners fed in these places that numbers of them refused to partake of nourishment until a more humane treatment had been introduced ; some resolved to die of starvation, others had food forced down their throats. Cumulative irritations like these worked minds up to a pitch of frenzy. On the 2d (14th) of August, 1878, Kavalsky was shot at Odessa by order of a military tribunal. Two days later, in retaliation, General Mesentsev, chief of the Third Section, was stabbed to death in the Nevsky Prospect in full daylight. The reply of the government was to hand over all political crimes of violence to a military tribunal, to strengthen the spy and repressive system, and to appeal to society for aid and sympathy. A few months after the murder of Mesentsev, the police broke up the Zemlya i Volya Society. It was promptly reorganized. Student demonstrations followed in several of the university towns. The pro vincial assemblies began to talk Liberalism. Otherwise, society seemed bound hand and foot. Fear of the spy chilled conversation in the most harmless gatherings. General Drenteln, suc- ceeding Mesentsev, cast nearly two thousand persons into prison in St. Petersburg alone.[1] In February, 1879, Prince Krapotkin, governor of Kharkov, was shot by Goldenberg for ill treat- ing prisoners under his care. Two months later, on the 2d (14th) of April, 1879, came Soloviev's attempt on the life of the emperor. The would- be assassin fired five shots at the Tsar, but none of them took effect. Absolutism now fully awakened to its danger. The country was di- vided into six divisions, and a general governor, armed with extraordinary powers, detailed to each. The pass system was enforced with new rigors. In St. Petersburg, General Gurko con- verted the *dvorniki,* or house porters, into a body of spies charged with regular police duty.

---

[1] An attack upon Drenteln precipitated the abolition of the "Third Section," but that organization was speedily reëstablished under another name.

The reply of the revolt was characteristic. In, the summer of 1879 a congress of socialists, revolutionists, and terrorists met at Voronezh, and there a terroristic activity was formally resolved upon. The terrible " Executive Committee " came into existence. Early in August sentence of death was passed upon the Tsar. The conspirators were thoroughly in earnest. Three mines were laid in anticipation of the emperor's return journey from the Crimea: one at Moscow, the second at Odessa, and another in Alexandrovsk. All the attempts failed. The Moscow explosion, which had been carefully prepared by Hartmann, Sophie Peróvskaya, Goldenberg, and others, occurred prematurely. The scene of action was then transferred to St. Petersburg. Khalturin, obtaining service in the Winter Palace as decorator, stored dynamite beneath the dining-hall; the explosion thus prepared took place on the 5th (17th) of February, 1880. Ten men of the watch were killed and fifty-three wounded. The emperor, delayed in going to table, had again escaped. In a proclamation which followed the Executive Committee expressed regret at the death of innocent soldiers, but declared the determination of the instigators to continue their struggle until they had won a constitutional form of government for the country. The party of the

"People's Will" had, in the mean time, come into existence. In 1880 a new and formidable organization, with the Executive Committee at its head, arose to carry into effect the sentence passed at Voronezh. It was a system of independent decentralized circles, destructible as single entities, but collectively invulnerable: forming a chain of influences without visible connecting links; offering to members the maximum of scope for enterprise with the minimum of danger; worked by conspirators unknown to each other; and wielded by officially invisible leaders empowered to visit disobedience with the punishment of death. Early in the year 1881 the preparations were completed. The emperor was to return from a review dinner on the 1st (13th) of March, 1881. He had the choice of three routes; one over the "Stone Bridge," another through the Malaya Sadovaya (Little Garden) Street, a third along the Yekaterinsky Canal. The bridge and the street were mined. The Tsar returned by the canal. To the conspirators in waiting Sophie Peróvskaya gave the signal by waving her handkerchief. Ryssakov's bomb shattered the imperial carriage; the bomb thrown by Grinevsky killed the emperor.

A month later Zheliabov, Peróvskaya, Kibalshchich, Michailov, and Ryssakov suffered the

14

penalty of death. The actual assassin, Grinevsky, had been killed by the explosion. Upon Hesse Helfmann the capital sentence was not carried out. A reign of terror followed the event of the 13th of March. The coronation of Alexander III. had to be put off for two years, the new emperor temporarily retreating for greater safety to Gatchina. The terrorists in the mean time continued their deadly activity. In March, 1882, Strelnikov, military *procureur* of Odessa, was fired at and killed. Late in December, 1883, Colonel Sudeikin, a zealous and not over-scrupulous police agent, fell assassinated in the Nevsky Prospect. During the past eighteen months numerous conspiracies, some of them aiming at regicide, have been brought to light. At the time of writing, an extensive propaganda has the army for its sphere of operation; agrarian outbreaks and risings are also being fomented in the south and west.

During the last thirty years there have been one hundred and thirty-five political prosecutions in Russia, involving the arrest and punishment of 1356 persons. Of these a very large number were sentenced to hard labor in the mines or banished for life to Siberia. Forty-five of the accused were either shot or hung: five in the reign of Nicholas, thirty-one under Alexander II., and nine in the reign of the present emperor. During the same period about fifty political prisoners met their death by violence in the gaols, or while serving a sentence of banishment. Between 1878 and 1882 the police shot eight persons during demonstrations, arrests, etc. Three others took their own lives in order to avoid falling into the hands of the authorities. The number of persons thrown into prison or banished without preliminary trial, under the so-called " administrative procedure," is very large, but cannot be stated with any degree of certainty. During the past twenty years about two hundred persons fled from prisons or places of banishment; most of them succeeded in reaching western Europe. [1]

[2] For a mass of information concerning the dynamic phases of the revolt, see the *Calendar of the People's Will* (in Russian). For readers of German, Professor Thun's *Geschichte der revolutionären Bewegungen in Russland* will be found useful.

PERSONAL CHARACTERISTICS.

THUS far the reader has looked merely upon the external features of the dynamic protest against absolutism in Russia. The revolt had an inner, psychological side, best shown, perhaps, by a glance at the personalities engaged in it. These may be divided into two classes. The first includes what I shall call the literary forces of the revolt; to the second belong its dynamic activities. The former category will be described in a single illustration. Instead of again going over the partly-told story of the career of Herzen, who spent most of his life abroad; or of giving an account of Bakunin, who was an international rather than a Russian agitator, I shall direct the reader's attention to the *littérateur* of the revolt, *par excellence*, Chernishevsky, a man of the people, who labored for his countrymen on the soil from which they sprang, and whose memory is indissolubly linked with predecessors in common with whom he spent the best years of his life in that grave of Russian genius, Siberia.

Nikolai Gavrilovich Chernishevsky was born at Saratov in the year 1829. His father, a priest at the local cathedral, was a man of intellectual gifts, remarkable for his honesty and uprightness, an affectionate parent, and a warm friend. The boy received his preliminary education at the Saratov Ecclesiastical Seminary, and was thence transferred to the university of St. Petersburg, where, a student in its Philological Faculty, he applied himself with great ardor and success to the acquirement of the Latin, Greek, and Slavic tongues. Later, he gave his attention to socialistic science, in which field his great receptivity, singular perseverance, and superior memory quickly ranked him as an authority even amongst specialists. Chernishevsky completed his university course in 1850, and thereupon became professor of literature to the first corps of cadets. This post he gave up after the lapse of a year in response to the urgent entreaties of his mother, who had a strong affection for her son and desired his presence in Saratov. Once more in his native town Chernishevsky became a teacher in the local gymnasium. He occupied in his father's house an apartment looking out on the Volga; here he received his friends, and gathered round him a circle of young people who became both his pupils and his admirers. He married in 1853, the same year in which his mother died. Returning to St. Petersburg with his wife, Nikolai Gavrilovich found himself in the capital without a copek. Happily for both, his courage did not desert him. His first effort to keep the wolf from the door resulted in a feat which only a Russian would have attempted, and probably only a Russian could have accomplished. Driven to translation, this born linguist acquired sufficient English in two months to be able at the end of that space of time to begin publication in the "Annals of the Fatherland" of a Russian version of a novel issued in London. From mere hack work he soon rose to the position of essay writer and critic, later winning renown by a brilliant dissertation on "The æsthetic relation of art to reality." It was this effort which led to Chernishevsky's appointment as *collaborateur* on the staff of the liberal review, "Sovremennik" (Contemporary), — a position which, affording as it did the fullest scope for the critic's rare intellectual gifts, gave Nikolai Gavrilovich the opportunity for which he had long been waiting. Nothing could excel the tact and ability with which he now applied himself to the task of popularizing the new ideas. Essay after essay issued from his pen, each full of the rich results of Western economical science. The views of Malthus and

the teachings of John Stuart Mill he made almost as familiar to his countrymen as they were
to English readers of the time; his papers on
agriculture and land-holding in Russia were of
especial value and interest. By all classes his
writings were eagerly and widely read, and as
a natural consequence they began to attract the
attention of the government. "At that time,"
said Chernishevsky to the writer, in Astrakhan,
more than twenty years afterwards, "I was
not more — if it be permitted to compare a
small man with great ones — than a sort of Russian Cobden or Bright. I did not, moreover,
always express my own ideas. I had to do a
good deal of hack work in literature, and my
position compelled me to live by my pen."
Modest as was this ambition, it was too much
for the Russia of those days. A charge was
trumped up against Chernishevsky of having,
amongst other things, prepared a proclamation
calling upon the peasants of the crown to revolt; and upon evidence very unreliable and inadequate, this promising *littérateur* was first
imprisoned in St. Petersburg for two years, and
then sentenced to fourteen years' hard labor in
Siberia, with subsequent banishment for life as
a colonist. Such was the cost of trying to be a
Cobden or a Bright in Russia! Yet Chernishevsky did not lose heart. It was the lot of

this remarkable man to exert his influence over
minds in Russia under conditions which would
have made the career of his English models
well-nigh impossible. They possessed constitutional means of agitating ; Chernishevsky had
none. Bright and Cobden had public plat-
forms from which to speak openly to the people ; Chernishevsky could not talk freely in the
circle of his own intimate friends without ap-
prehension of giving offense to the government
through the ears of the ubiquitous police spy.
Everything and every one seemed to conspire
against Chernishevsky becoming a power. It
was he who had to give painful birth to his
socialistic doctrines under the very eye of the
censor, he who was compelled to produce his
chef d'œuvre not in a gilded saloon of the
Nevsky Prospect, but in the cheerless seclusion
of a St. Petersburg prison. Yet the man
wielded an influence widespread and extraordinary. Scarcely had he been cast into prison before he began the composition of a work which
was destined to add enormously to the number
of his followers. It was the famous romance
"What's to be done ?" The success of this
book — tediously prolix and inartistic as a literary composition — was mainly due to its socialism, its idealistic views of life, and its hints
rather than schemes for the reorganization of

labor and of society. Written anonymously for the "Contemporary," artfully constructed to evade condemnation by the censor, and suggesting much to be read between the lines, the novel achieved a fair reputation in the periodical press before its real tendencies were discovered. Prohibition came at last, and insured, as it usually does in Russia, the complete success of the thing prohibited. Since then, public taste has gone far ahead of "What's to be done?" yet the censor cannot even in 1885 find in his heart to "permit" the volume, even as a literary curiosity.

At last Chernishevsky was taken from his cell in the Fortress of Peter and Paul at St. Petersburg, and transferred to the place of his exile and hard labor. For nineteen years he disappeared from Europe and from civilization. What were his thoughts during that long period? How he suffered and in what way, who can tell? From 1864 to 1871 he was kept at a station in the Zabaikal province, Eastern Siberia; from 1871 to 1883 he was detained at Viluisk, a town on the river Vilui, not far from Yakutsk. On one occasion an attempt was made to rescue him, but Chernishevsky could not be roused from the lethargic despair into which he had fallen. The government allowed nothing to transpire concerning their prisoner;

in the end, the exile became a mystery, and the source of all kinds of rumors. In 1880 literary Europe heard of his death; in 1881 Herr Ulbach asked the Vienna Literary Congress to petition the late Tsar for the man's release; just before the death of Alexander II. the St. Petersburg journal " Strana " received a first warning for having called upon the government to allow Chernishevsky's return to Europe.

In the autumn of 1883, to the surprise of all, Chernishevsky was transferred from Siberia to Astrakhan by virtue of an imperial pardon, forming one of the " concessions " of the Coronation Manifesto. Being in Astrakhan by a mere coincidence when he entered Europe, I was the first European, not a Russian or a government official, to see him on his return. At first he seemed to me broad-shouldered, stronglimbed and active, looking at fifty-five fully ten years younger. A second glance showed him to be nervously restless in his manner, in a state bordering on mental prostration, a complete myope. He received me warmly, and we conversed together for more than an hour. What he told me of his experiences in exile has already been published;[1] there are other and special reasons why I do not repeat it here. The story may have been reliable enough, so

---

[1] *Daily News*, December 22, 1883.

far as it went, yet the fact that it was told
"in the toils"—at Astrakhan rather than at
Paris or London — deprives it of historic value.
Nineteen years' experience of Russian exile
poorly qualifies a man of shattered nerves and
impaired physical health for any formidable in-
dictment of a government upon whose "clem-
ency" he depends not only for the smallest
comforts of life, but for the right to exist itself.
And when such a man has courage enough to
admit that he was once put into chains, —
"against the wishes of the government," — the
reader may easily fill up the gaps of a narra-
tive like that told to me. Such, then, was our
interview. I have already indicated the short-
ness of its duration. Disturbed by the constant trepidations of the ex-exile's faithful wife,
watched over from without by that body of
spies who still hold Chernishevsky, "pardoned"
by the Russian government, the prisoner of the
Russian police, we at last decided to separate.
Before taking leave of me Chernishevsky placed
in my hand a small volume, in a blank page of
which he had linked our names with the words,
"In memory of our acquaintance, Astrakhan,
1883." On our rising to say good-by, Madame
Chernishevsky entered the room, and with a
hasty movement of solicitude threw her arms
around her husband, as if to shield him from

some impending peril, — tears the meanwhile choking her utterance. He gently unclasped her hands, stroked her forehead caressingly, and having uttered a few words of affectionate consolation, kissed her. " She is so afraid ! " said Chernishevsky in explanation. Then I took my departure.

Let us now glance at the organizers and conspirators of the revolt in its dynamic period. Of these none was more remarkable than Sophie Lvovna Peróvskaya, who belonged to one of the most aristocratic families in Russia. One of her ancestors was the morganatic husband of the Empress Elizabeth Petrovna. Her grandfather was Minister of Public Instruction ; her father, General Governor of St. Petersburg. Sophie Lvovna was born in the capital in the year 1854. Strongly attached to her mother, who loved her much in return, she had a peculiar aversion for her father, who is described as a *chinovnik*, full of the pettiness and self-seeking of his class. Her education began at the age of eight and continued for six years. In 1869 the family returned to St. Petersburg from the Crimea. She at once entered the women's class of a gymnasium, and there formed the acquaintance of Sophie Loschern, Kornilova, and others, all of whom afterwards took part in the propaganda. On her father

forbidding the visits of these acquaintances
Sophie Lvovna left home never to return.
Eager for knowledge, she next joined the Chaikovtsy Society, — at first a literary, afterwards
a political organization, — and began an earnest
study of social and political questions. While
qualifying herself as a school-teacher, she became acquainted with the writings of Chernishevsky and Dobrolyubov; for the famous
"Shto Dyelat?" (What's to be done?) of the
former, she entertained an enthusiastic admiration. Prepared at last for "going to the people," she set out on her pilgrimage, traversing
the whole course of the Lower Volga in pursu-
ance of her mission. Hardships under which
a peasant woman would have sunk, she bore
with the greatest resolution, even cheerfulness.
Her food was mostly milk and roots; her bed
rarely anything more than a sack filled with
straw. In 1872 she had reached Kama, near
the Ural range, and was wandering from village to village, endeavoring to awaken the people to a knowledge of their lot. We next see
her in Tver, aiding the cause of the revolt as a
school-teacher. Late in 1873 she returned to
St. Petersburg. Her arrest followed, but after
a year spent in prison she was set at liberty
owing to want of evidence. For three years
she remained under police surveillance. This

space of time she utilized in acquiring a knowledge of the healing art; her diploma was obtained after a regular course at a medical school in Simpheropol. In 1877 the members of the Chaikovtsy Society, to the number of one hundred and ninety-three, found themselves in the hands of the police, charged with political conspiracy. After a long trial the jury set Sophie Lvovna at liberty, but the authorities banished her "administratively" to the northern government of Olonets. On the way thither she escaped from her guards, concealed herself for six hours in a wood, and then made her way back to St. Petersburg. Soon afterwards she took part, as leader, in various attempts to rescue conspirators by force from the custody of the police. At Kharkov she headed a band disguised as gendarmes. In 1879 she actively assisted in preparing the famous mine at Moscow. Later she helped to organize the "Narodnaya Volya" (People's Will) party. Her last act as a conspirator was to give the signal for the assassination of Alexander II.

Sophie Lvovna's personality has been described at great length. With an extraordinary capacity for conspiracy and organization, she remained a woman, yet was in some respects a mere child. At twenty-six she looked not more than eighteen. Her features were strikingly

open, her face oval, her forehead singularly
high. The eyes were blue and the complexion
blonde. To many, her whole aspect was that of
personified youth. She laughed heartily when
provoked to merriment, dressed simply, and
like most Russian women held uncleanliness
in horror. Her liking for children was great;
as an attendant on the sick she was unsur-
passed.

Her relations with Varvara Sergeiyevna, her
mother, were of the tenderest kind. To see
this parent, the daughter frequently risked her
life. She was particularly sensitive of Varvara's anxiety on her account, and did all in
her power to allay it. At last, under final
arrest and awaiting a sentence that was to send
her to the scaffold, she wrote to her mother
what must be called one of the most eloquent
and solemn and touching epistles ever composed
in anticipation of death.

My darling, my priceless mother [it began],
the thought of how it is with thee pains and torments me continually. My dear one, I implore thee,
calm thyself, spare thyself, and do not be troubled in
mind, not only for the sake of those who surround
thee, but also for my sake. Not for a moment do I
sorrow concerning my fate; I look forward to it
calmly, for I have long known and anticipated that
it would end thus. And this fate is, after all, dear

mother, not so terrible. I have lived as my convictions dictated; contrary to them I could not act; therefore I await with a calm conscience all that impends for me. One thing only weighs upon me like a heavy burden; and it is thy sorrow, my precious mother. That is all that troubles me; if I could only lighten thy pain there is nothing that I would not give. But remember, my darling [1] mother, that thou hast a large family about thee, and that to the children who surround thee thou art necessary as a model of moral strength. In my inmost soul I have always regretted that I could never attain to that moral height whereon thou standest; yet in certain moments of doubt, thy image has always sustained me. I shall not assure thee of my affection, for thou knowest that from my earliest childhood thou hast been the object of my continual and most sublime love. Concern regarding thee was always for me a great pain. My darling, I hope thou wilt calm thyself, and to some extent, at least, forgive me for all the sorrow I am bringing thee. I hope that thou wilt not blame me too severely. Thy reproach is the only thing that can oppress me. Passionately, passionately, in imagination, I kiss thy dear hands, and on my knees I implore thee not to be angry with me. Give my warm greeting to all my relatives. I have only one more request to make, dearest mother; buy me a collar and gloves with buttons ; . . . one must prepare one's costume for the tribunal. Till we meet again, my

---

[1] The expression used in the original is " golubonka "— a word hardly translatable, literally " dear little dove."

darling, I repeat my prayer. Do not be angry and
do not trouble thyself about me. My fate is not so
sad, after all, and it beseems not that thou shouldst
mourn for me. Thy   SONYA.[1]

March 22 (April 3), 1881.

On receiving this letter, the mother hastened
to the prison in which her daughter was confined. Permission to see her was refused from
day to day down to the very hour of execution.
At last the mother had the terrible consolation
of seeing her child driven away to the place of
slaughter on an open tumbril, in the midst of
those companions from whom she had implored
the judges not to separate her.

Andrei Zheliabov, one of the five who perished in the Semenovsky Field, was born a
serf in the Krim in 1850. His grandfather,
a sectarian, taught him Ecclesiastical Slavonic,
and made him learn the psalter by heart. Soon
Andrei attracted the attention of his owner,
who gave him lessons in Russian and finally
sent him to school at Kerch. He entered Odessa
University as a student in 1868, but was ex-
pelled for having joined in a demonstration
against a professor. Zheliabov thenceforward
had to support himself by giving lessons. At
first he spent his leisure in organizing students'
associations, libraries, etc.; tiring of this sphere

[1] Diminutive of "Sophie."

15

of activity, he joined a political society formed in Odessa about the time of the Nechayev conspiracy. In this connection he became very popular amongst his comrades. In 1872 he became member of an organization affiliated with the Chaikovtsy Society, and later in that capacity took part in the movement "to the people." One of his disguises as a propagandist was that of a vegetable-seller. But his ambition rose above the work of explaining socialism to peasants, or distributing revolutionary literature in workshops and factories. Zheliabov was a born organizer and leader; a man of deed rather than word, yet eloquent and persuasive in an emergency; easily angered by insult or ridicule, he had a pleasing manner, and was a favorite in society. Zheliabov approved of all the measures likely to further the cause of the revolt. Tsarism, the unlimited power of a single individual wielded over a whole people, — this he hated and opposed with all the intensity of feeling of which his passionate nature was capable. The news of Karakasov's shot he received, when only a boy of fifteen, with an exclamation of delight. In 1877, involved in the Chaikovtsy prosecution, he spent seven months in prison as the penalty of his activity as a propagandist. In 1879 he entered the ranks of the terrorists, and was one of those who sentenced the Tsar to death at Voronezh. Immediately after the congress, he proceeded to the south of Russia and was there active in winning recruits, particularly in the university towns. As a speaker, his success was marked. His mastery of the subject in hand, the logical completeness of his arguments, his clear enunciation and professorial air, as well as his readiness at repartee, charmed many and convinced more. Late in 1879, Zheliabov, as agent of the Executive Committee, superintended the construction of the mine at Alexandrovsk, and after the triple failure, went to St. Petersburg, where he was appointed to the oversight of a number of dynamite factories. In the capital he gathered about him a number of young people who willingly accepted him as their guide and leader. His description of himself was that of a born demagogue, his proper place being, as he was accustomed to assure his friends, in the street, in the middle of a crowd of workmen. Zheliabov had great fondness for literature. It is related of him that "Tarass Bulba," Gogol's celebrated story, so fascinated him that he could not close the book until he had lost a night of sleep in reading it through. "Others will rise up after us" was his unvarying reply to prognostications of personal disaster. In Zheliabov's faith the cause would live, though the individuals might perish.   The prosecuting attorney said of him, during the trial which ended in the quintuple sentence of death : " Zheliabov was a remarkably typical conspirator in everything, — in gestures, in mimicry, in movement, in idea, and in language, — and did all with a certain theatrical effect.   To the last moment he remained robed in his conspiratorial toga.'   It is impossible to deny to him the possession of talent and cleverness."

Nikolai Kibalshchich, born in 1854, was the son of a priest stationed in a village of the Chernigov government.   In 1871 he studied at the School for Engineers, two years later joining the Medical Academy in St. Petersburg. His first collision with the authorities occurred in 1875.   He had casually undertaken to take charge of a packet of revolutionary publications for a friend living in constant dread of a domiciliary visitation, and on the police selecting the house of Kibalshchich for their attentions, they found the incriminating literature in his possession.   He was kept in prison for three years, the whole of which time he devoted to study ; his very " exercise " promenades are said to have been utilized in the task of winning his fellow-prisoners over to the cause of the revolt. He was a man of strongly phlegmatic temperament; his manner was reserved, his speech slow, and his moods so equable that it was impossible to say when he was pleased or when in anger. Only once was he warmed into visible enthusiasm. It was when his comrades told him of a plot against the imperial family. Set at liberty, Kibalshchich at once began the study of explosives, and knowing French, German, and English, quickly mastered all that was to be learned about mines, bombs, and the like. He had a whole laboratory fitted up for his experiments; became the chemist, the technologist of terrorism, and finally prepared those instruments of death which were thrown on the 13th of March.

Grinevsky, who killed the Tsar and was hoist by his own petard, was a Pole, born in the government of Minsk in the year 1856. His family lived in the greatest poverty. The boy was a diligent scholar. In contact with comrade students at Bialystock, Grinevsky imbibed socialistic views, and had devoted himself to the service of the people long before his educational course was at an end. In 1875 he went to St. Petersburg, and there joined the pupils of the Technological Institute. His activity in the capital was marked. He established a secret society, collected money for exiles, fabricated passports, and at last went to the people with the rest. On his return, disappointed and discouraged, he joined the terrorists.

Such were four of the personalities who aided in carrying the revolt into its dynamic phase. They represented strata of society utterly removed from each other in many ways ; for one was born an aristocrat, the second came into the world a slave, the third was the son of a priest, and the fourth a student in the schools. Yet they were all united in an intense love of their country, in a sorrow for its suffering people, and a hatred of tyranny and oppression that made actions immoral in themselves seem to them the highest virtue ; and all of them alike met death, not with the selfish circumspection of the conspirator who makes success conditional on his own safety, but with the sublime recklessness of men and women who, however misguided in their choice of methods, yet gladly offer their lives for the cause which they believe to be sacred and true.

MODERN IRRITATIONS.

Such has been the history of the revolt. It began in an unscrupulous negation of the racial spirit and traditions; in the gradual destruction of individual and communal liberties; in the forcible unification of tribes and territories that stood naturally apart; in the wresting from the people, by force of ambition and arms, those privileges of self-government which they have never yielded up, and which they claim to this day; in the establishment of an absolutism repugnant to the national temper and genius, inconsistent with its early history, irreconcilable with its modern civilization. To these original causes must also be added a long series of irritations extending from the earliest days of Tsarism down to the present time. Intensified by domestic tyranny, stimulated not less powerfully by agrarian enslavement, the revolt became more bitter with every increase in the burdens which the growing state cast upon the individual. At first passive, or only indirectly dynamic, it soon assumed, under the stimulus of

Western culture, the character of propaganda
and declared resistance to authority; finally we
see it developed, under cruel methods of reprisal
and repression, into a system of organized violence and terrorism.

The revolt has its foundation of historic discontent, and yet draws much of its modern intensity from irritations and conditions that have
been created by absolutism itself. No one can
live long in Russia without finding himself surrounded by an atmosphere strangely wanting in
restrictive social influences. In the west of
Europe the individual is subordinated, in spite
of himself, to the conceptions and canons and
systems of society at large. In Russia, an extraordinary scope for doing unusual things in
politics, religion, and morals takes the place of
subservience to cumulative prejudices and traditions. The striking characteristic of Russian
society is that it is held together by no bond of
union at all valid for the regulation of personal
conduct. It seems as though historical as well as
geographical conditions had developed the individual, at the expense of the social, sentiment.
And this want of social solidarity, setting individualism free to act out its own desires and
caprices, often blinding it to the general interests of the social mass, has been intensified by
the very power which ought to have striven for

its removal. Fearing all union of thought, all intercommunication of idea, all free groupings and assimilations of the intellectual elements of the national life, the Russian government has brought its repressive measures to bear upon the very machinery by which, in other countries, society hedges its individual elements around with a healthy moral control. There is nothing more needed in Russia than a public conscience ; this the government has destroyed, or rather rendered impossible.

Various instruments have been employed to cripple the social sentiment in Russia. Not the least powerful of them is that of the censorship. Just as in every theatre in Russia there is a *loge* reserved for the chief of police, so in every Russian newspaper office there is a silent presence, ever holding in check the pen, if not the thought, of the unhappy journalist whose duty it is to write on "the topics of the day." Between the years 1865 and 1880 the Press Council had given one hundred and sixty-seven warnings and suspended fifty-two newspapers. In the year 1882 five journals were suspended ; five others received a first warning, three a second, and one a third ; from six the privilege of street sale was withdrawn. Journals indispensable to healthy social development, like the "Den," the "Moskva," the "Grazhdanin,"

"Trud," "Poriadok," and the "Golos," have one by one succumbed to censorial severity until to-day the Russians have scarcely an independent, certainly no outspoken liberal, organ left. The case of the "Otechestvenny Zapiski" (Annals of the Fatherland), suppressed last year, affords a striking illustration of the condition of journalism in Russia. The editor of that review, the celebrated Prince Saltykov, better known by his *nom de guerre* of "Shchedrin," had brought into existence a new kind of journalism suited to the exigencies of censorship on the one hand, and to the character of his own satirical talent on the other. He wrote mainly tales. They were like clippings from Boccaccio, just as light, just as witty, just as immoral. It was like a Russian Heine imitating the "Decameron" in Slavonic. The aim of the writer was to show that so long as political topics were avoided almost any excesses might be indulged in. And the experiment was thoroughly successful, for Shchedrin succeeded in putting before his public sketches revolting in their lewdness; such as, in any other country than Russia, would have brought upon their author the punishment of the criminal law.[1]

[1] The *Annals* was suppressed, the reader may remember, not for its indecency, to which the censor paid no (official) attention, but for its "dangerous" political opinions, and the alleged connection of members of its staff with secret societies.

The evil of censorship is multifold. It not only prevents the formation of healthy public sentiment; it discourages thinking; by trammeling expression, it makes journalism frivolous; it forms a serious hindrance to educational processes, and by menacing them with heavy losses makes newspaper enterprises the most precarious of all. Peculiarly vexatious, moreover, are the restrictions upon the reading of foreign books, since they not only deprive the studious classes of valuable and urgently needed knowledge, but make an invidious distinction in favor of *chin,* or rank. A general, or his hierarchical equivalent, may read a book like Zola's "Nana" with impunity, yet the poor student consults his borrowed scientific treatise or religious essay in fear and trembling. Young men often spend the whole of their leisure time, for months together, in copying volumes which they can only handle at the risk of being dealt with as readers of "forbidden literature." While in St. Petersburg I saw a copy of the French work "Jesus-Buddha" produced under strangely mediæval conditions. The owner of the original was an army general, who had the full right of his rank to peruse the book, but had pronounced it "dry reading" and handed it over to a friend uncut; the copy belonged to a young medical student, who was precluded by his want of the needed *chin* from even buying the work, but had taken so serious an interest in the volume as to consider five months well spent in its transcription !

Another condition highly favorable to the revolt is the absence from Russian life of all those specialized activities which citizenship involves in countries governed constitutionally. For the purely social effects of this kind of emptiness one need only glance at the literary pictures which Gogol has left his countrymen, — at the petty aspirations and miserable interests of characters like Ivan Ivanovich and Ivan Nikephoróvich, with their lifelong feud over an old gun ; like the *chinovnik* Akaky Akakyevich, the single ambition of whose existence was to have a new coat ; or Perigov, the officer, whose field of glory was the Nevsky Prospect, whenever he could pace it at the fashionable hour in full military uniform, with a sword scabbard dangling at his heels. The results of political emptiness are seen in the revolt itself. The need of playing a part in politics, of aspiring to office or power, however petty that power may be, of organizing something, conducting something, championing something, — this is so strong in modern civilization that if it be suppressed for one side or phase of life, it is sure to find satisfaction and fulfillment on another. The energy, the talent for organization, the natural leadership and acquired discipline about which one hears so much in nihilistic literature, are simply so many qualities that have been diverted from their proper spheres of immediate public usefulness into activities of conspiracy and propaganda and terrorism. Even the intellectual exercise of popular assemblies gathered to discuss public affairs is denied to the Russian people. Hence, while there is no career for the political orator, the success of the clandestine demagogue is assured; while political parties are prohibited and unknown, secret societies everywhere draw vitality from the open aid or tacit sympathy of the people; while the existing system calls no national representatives together for constitutional purposes, delegates converge from all the provinces to sanction the dread proposals of the Executive Committee.

Revolt seems natural, sedition innate in the Russian capital. Its luminous summer midnights tend to mental irritation; its long winter evenings favor conspiracy. Its populations seem continually hiding from each other in the hearts of immense tetragons of brick and stone, vast as the quadrangles which they inclose. Thousands of aspiring young men and women journey annually to St. Petersburg, and there lead a life free from the slightest parental restraint. An unhealthy atmosphere, a variety of maladies, the daily spectacle of the most abject and terrible forms of poverty side by side with that of the most ostentatious and self-complacent wealth, are of themselves sufficient, without natural predilection or political grievance, to prompt to pessimistic views of life. The students are sometimes all but paupers themselves, and not a few owe their education and their prospects wholly to the bounty of the government. When pinched in resources, they must be content to occupy the smallest of rooms in the biggest of buildings; sometimes not more than the corner of an apartment falls to their lot during the hours of sleep. Students have been known to prepare their lessons by the light of the staircase or street lamp in order to save the cost of a candle, or to walk several miles in order to give a lesson for a midday meal. And when sorry resources like these fail, one sees in the newspapers such appeals as " Wanted, something to do, anywhere and for anything; " " Here's half a year gone, and I 've got nothing yet; " or " For the love of God keep a blind student and his family from starvation ! " [1]

The Greek Church merely extends without strengthening the surface exposed by absolutism to the assaults of the revolt. The close union

---

[1] Literally translated from the *Golos.*

of Tsarism and Orthodoxy, strengthened in some recent cases to the point of conferring functions of police espionage upon the clergy, fails to disguise the relaxing hold of the church upon the masses of the people. Ignorance, drunkenness, and greed of wealth continue to be the vices of the priesthood, as intellectual stagnation, unbroken by a single fundamental reform, continues to be the fatal weakness of the national religion. "All the information and evidence obtainable," runs the report of an imperial commission appointed to consider the state of the people in 1873, "shows that the influence of the clergy is in a continual state of decadence. The priesthood is little imbued with the sacredness of its mission; it presents not the slightest example of morality. . . . In Simbersk, Pensa, Samara, and Ufa, there is a falling off in the performance of religious duties amongst the peasantry: the causes are the small moral influence of the clergy, the absence of all civil and religious instruction, and the influence of the dram-shop." For the church to become the genuine church of the people, it must be divorced from Tsarism and reformed. The change wrought by the *raskol* in the days of Nikon left untouched its constitutions, rites, and language, which are consequently the same now as they were a thousand

years ago. To adapt the church of Vladimir
to the popular needs of modern Russia would
require an ecclesiastical re-birth. To maintain
it in its present condition ; to keep the monks
in their idle and luxurious uselessness, the white
clergy in the contempt of the people, and the
whole functions of religious ministration in an
atmosphere of meaningless formality and petty
commercialism, — this is simply to aid the cause
of the revolt.

The problem of reconciling absolutism with
European civilization is still further complicated by the increasing discontent of the agricultural classes. The sentimental satisfaction
which was conveyed to outsiders by the *ukaz*
of 1861 did not save peasants from the practical results of the legislation which made them
free cultivators. It not only lessened their
share of land, but in many cases raised the
government charges upon it to a rate out of all
proportion to the annual yield. Instead of giving the agriculturist his freedom, it brought him
under the jurisdiction of the new commune.
In a fiscal sense the peasant was just as firmly
attached to the glebe as he had ever been since
the days of Boris Godunov. Where the land
is poor, and agrarian operations require favorable conditions for their success, the tillers of
the soil live a life of abject poverty and, over-

burdened with commercial and state charges, fall an easy prey to avaricious money-lenders. The land-owning nobles have also suffered seriously from the new conditions imposed upon agriculture by the Act of 1861. In the province of Moscow alone, emancipation has thrown four fifths of the land out of cultivation in fifteen years.

The much lauded judicial reform is almost a dead letter. It has been paralyzed by modifications. In thirty-nine provinces out of the seventy-two the old courts are still maintained. "The examining magistrates," writes Prince Krapotkin,[1] "never enjoyed the independence bestowed on them by the new law; the judges have been made more and more dependent upon the Minister of Justice, whose nominees they are, and who has the right of transferring them from one province to another; the institution of sworn advocates, uncontrolled by criticism, has degenerated absolutely; and the peasant whose case is not likely to become a *cause célèbre* does not receive the benefit of counsel, and is completely in the hands of a creature like the *procureur-impérial* in Zola's novel."

Most serious of all, perhaps, are the irritations of the police system, not only on account

---

[1] *Nineteenth Century*, January, 1883.

of their sensational elements, but because they appeal to the sympathies and impulses. Nothing is so well calculated to intensify the dynamic character of the revolt as the punitive measures devised by the authorities for its suppression. The practice of administrative exile, whereby thousands of people were banished to Siberia without trial, — without even the formality of communicating the cause of disappearance to their relatives, — was continued up to the year 1881, and only then mitigated to the extent of handing such cases over to a special commission for its approbation, and of limiting the banishment to a term of five years. The process still goes on, and retains all the secret character which before made it obnoxious; the check imposed simply prevents banishment for private, that is, for other than political causes. Hence the old questions arise in every exigency of public excitement. Who are taken, and whither? What is the offense, and who are the judges? Who prosecute? What is the punishment? The number dealt with in this fashion is enormous. Under Loris Melikov it reached 1696, under Ignatiev it was 2836! Nor do these figures take account of the other method of dealing administratively with prisoners, by which the authorities are empowered to take an accused who has been acquitted by a jury and punish him secretly as they see fit. Is it any wonder that society should be restive under this suspended sword of police machinery that, often without more pretext than the discovery of an "illegal" publication in a letter-box, or weightier testimony than that of a paid or otherwise interested denunciator, may now cut off a man or woman from family, home, and country for life? It asks for new processes resting upon righteous laws of evidence, for other forms of judicial procedure more European. Above all, it claims for every political prisoner or person now dealt with "administratively" the right to a public trial.

But what will the reader think of Russian methods of treating political prisoners after they have been lodged in gaol or sent into exile? Not very long ago M. Paul Birvansky, an imperial state attorney, was sent upon a special mission to Orenburg by the Minister of Justice, with orders to investigate and report upon the practice of the imperial tribunals in that province. He remained absent on his mission four months, and his experiences were published in the "Syeverny Vyestnik," (Northern Messenger):—

During my four months' inquiry [he wrote], it was revealed to me how our judges trample the laws

under foot; how cynical and wanton is the behavior
of our police; how savagely brute force is brought to
bear upon the weak and friendless. I lived in an atmosphere of appalling groans and heart-breaking
sighs. I liberated innocent persons who had been
kept in prison by the executive several years after
they had been publicly acquitted in open court, and
who had been secretly tortured. I took down the
depositions of peasant women who had been subjected
to torment — their flesh pinched with red-hot tongs
— by order and in the presence of the chief commis-
sary of police, merely because they had presumed to
plead on behalf of their unfortunate husbands. I
convinced myself that there was absolutely nothing
in common between myself and the local authorities.
A black and bottomless gulf lay between us. They
trafficked wantonly with our laws, converting them
into instruments of extortion. . . . Words fail me to
describe the impressions made upon me by my first
visit to the state prisons. Hundreds of human beings
find a premature grave in these loathsome dens. They
die lingering deaths therein, or emerge from them
crippled for life. . . . It was horrible to be compelled
to acknowledge to one's self that these semi-animate,
wasted, filthy, and dun-colored objects, draped in a
few rotten rags, were, after all, men and women. . . .
The confined atmosphere, poisoned by exhalations
from every sort of abomination, absolutely stopped
my breath, so rank and fetid was it. . . . I pass over
an infinite number of cases, each of which is horrible
enough to make your readers' hair stand on end, and

come to the last of all. I was making my customary
round of the district prisons when I noticed an abnormal excitement among the prisoners at Ilezk. The
gaol governor was also agitated and pale. I insti-
tuted an inquiry and found that two months pre-
viously all the prisoners had been led out to an open
space outside the town gates, and there beaten with
such inhuman cruelty that the populace wept bitterly
at the spectacle. . . . First they were flogged until
they lost consciousness; then water was poured over
them till they recovered; then the warders beat them
with whatever was readiest at hand, — belt buckles,
prison keys, iron chains, and the butt-ends of rifles.
The ground was stained with blood like the floor of
a shambles. Finally, the prisoners were tied together
with ropes by the feet and driven into the great court-
yard of the gaol, where they fell down from sheer
exhaustion into several bleeding and disfigured heaps,
scarcely recognizable as human beings."

Such is the statement not of a terrorist, or of
a prisoner, but of a Russian state official. It is
superfluous of course to add that M. Birvansky
was speedily dismissed from his functions at
Orenburg, and that for publishing his experiences the "Northern Messenger" was suspended.

The allegation that torture is still a part of
the Russian punitive system is supported by
statements scarcely less confident than that of
M. Birvansky. Prince Krapotkin declares that

at least two of the four who suffered death with Peróvskaya were tortured prior to their execution *by electricity,* in order to compel disclosures.[1]   It appears much more certain that Issayev was kept in a continual state of nervous excitement, with the alleged aim of provoking a confession.   Plotnikov, who had been in prison for years, in last extremes of weakness and ill-health, was thrown into chains for having one day ventured to declaim a verse of his favorite poet in the hearing of the gaoler.   Serekov, for neglecting to salute a guard placed over him, was put into a dark cage, so small that he could neither stand nor sit within, and had to maintain an attitude highly painful and exhausting. When Alexandrov sang a snatch of melody in an unguarded moment the gaoler struck him a blow in the face with his fist.   The gaol in which these occurrences took place is known as the Novobelgorod Central Prison, situated in the Volchansk district, about fifty-nine versts distant from the town of Kharkov.   A description of the place appeared in the "Moscow Telegraph" of the 6th (18th) of December, 1882.

[1] It is only fair to say that this allegation is denied in Russian official circles. The evidence upon which it was based is that of an eye-witness, who declared that at the place of execution Ryssakov showed his "mutilated hands" and said, "They have tortured us" (*muy pytali*). That these words were distinctly heard is very doubtful, since the authorities kept a band of music playing up to the last moment.

The writer spoke of the prison as "so over-crowded that the convicts lie one atop of another. The air in the cells is so impure that any one not accustomed to the place cannot remain inside for more than a few minutes. The boards which form the beds are frightfully unclean. . . . The prisoners themselves look ill and exhausted. They live in a state of the greatest nervous excitement. For punishment they are put for from one to seven days into small dark holes, in which a man can lie down only with the greatest difficulty."

The cells of the citadel (*ravelin*) prison in St. Petersburg are described as dark and cold as the grave. The walls drip with damp, and there are pools of water on the floor. The food given to the prisoners here consists of vegetable soup and bread. The place is warmed in winter once every three days ; every other day the prisoners are allowed to take exercise, that is, for a quarter of an hour each time. No reading or relaxation of any kind is permitted. The prisoners are closely watched. If one makes a movement with the head or hand, or only looks at something, the guard immediately jumps from his seat and asks the reason of the action. It was in this prison that Zubkovsky tried to make geometrical figures with his bread in order to practice geometry for relaxation, and had it taken away from him with the remark that hard labor convicts were not permitted to amuse themselves. Blows and the black hole are amongst the punishments awarded. It was here that Shiryaev fell into consumption; here that Okladsky and Tsukerman went mad; here that Martynovsky tried to commit suicide.

In the Kharkov prison political convicts are kept from three to five years in solitary confinement and in irons, in dark, damp cells that measure only ten feet by six, altogether isolated from intercourse with human beings. No books are allowed and no implements for manual labor. Shut up in places like these, Prince Krapotkin writes, prisoners "go rapidly to decay, and either descend calmly to the grave, or become lunatics. They do not go mad as, after being outraged by gendarmes, Miss M——, the promising young painter, did. She was bereft of reason instantly; her madness was simultaneous with her shame. Upon them insanity steals gradually and slowly; the mind rots in the body from hour to hour." In 1878 the prisoners at Kharkov, life having become insupportable, rebelled; six determined to starve themselves to death. For a week they refused to eat, and after terrible scenes arising from the attempt to feed them by injection, they were induced by delusive promises to take nourishment. Their demands were for regular warming of the cells, the provision of beds, exercise by twos instead of singly, placing of the lamp in the cell rather than in the corridor, and more humane treatment by the guard and officials in charge.

The lot of the political exile in Siberia is still more painful. "We live," writes a prisoner from Yakutsk, " literally in darkness, only having light for an hour and a half or two hours in order that we may see to eat. Our food is fish; we have no bread and cannot get meat. I thank you for the papers sent, but I have no money to buy candles, and therefore have n't the light to read by." Another writes, "My scorbutic ailment gets worse, and I only long now for death." "We work," says a third, " from six o'clock in the morning until eight o'clock at night in cold water that often reaches up to our knees. We leave work quite exhausted, and go to bed at once, for to read or converse is impossible. Last year (1881) we buried four of our comrades. Semyanovsky and Rodin committed suicide. Neizvestny and Krivozhyein died this year (1882). Kovalevskaya [1] went mad. The same fate awaits many more of us. We live in two narrow cells. We get no medical help. We need books, clothes, shoes, and

[1] Evidently a woman.

money. Our torments are frightful . . . . Farewell, dear friends, this is my last letter."   The prison referred to in this communication is known as the Nizhnaya Kara (Lower Kara). The political convicts confined therein numbered, at the beginning of 1884, about ninety. One of them describes the prison as dirty and damp.   "There is a physician, but he treats the sick so badly that they prefer not to ask his services.   It was he who had half-insane Kovalevskaya whipped nearly to death. . . . Armfeld was also beaten with a stick for simple impoliteness.   Zhutin died in his chains, bound to the wall. Kolenkin is on the point of death, owing to the wounds caused by his chains." [2]

Let me close this chapter with a word on the passport system, which must be described as one of the most harassing and widespread sources of all political irritation in modern Russia.   It

[2] A few of the statements here given are reproduced from the revolutionary organs, *Na Rodinyé* (At Home), *Narodnaya Volya* (Will of the People) and the *Chorny Peredyel* (Black Partition). The source is certainly partisan, yet it is the only source available, and so long as the Russian government restricts to adversaries the opportunity of collecting and disseminating information on this subject, so long will that information command the confidence and faith of the public. It is at any rate as much entitled to credence as the statements of some of those travelers who have enjoyed the honor of being "personally conducted" through the prison establishments of his highness the Tsar, but who have set out on their mission of exploration without the single indispensable requisite for that misssion, namely, a colloquial knowledge of Russian.

puts the population practically in the position
of convicts discharged on ticket-of-leave, and
compelled to report from time to time to the
police. If, on the one hand, it is a source of
revenue, yielding three million of rubles a year
or thereabouts, on the other it is a serious obstacle to freedom of motion and commercial development.   Nothing can terrify a peasant more than
the prospect of losing, or being refused his
" papers."   People have been known to commit
suicide rather than be found without a passport.
Not a few have been driven by their inability
to procure police certificates into secret socie-
eties, the members of which, for the most part,
live " illegally," that is to say, without passports, or on the strength of documents fabricated by themselves.   The police frequently
refuse passports to persons whom they suspect
of " political infidelity ;" this kind of terrorism
is a favorite form of ex-judicial persecution in
Russia.

EUROPE AND THE REVOLT: THE FUTURE.

THE conclusion that, under the existing *régime* in Russia, the revolt is a permanent element of the national life thus becomes inevitable. It is an essence, a nature of things, rather than a mere phenomenon. Its inner reality exists independently of its outer accident or form. Just as a mass of water may assume the character of a still lake, a rippling brook, a noisy waterfall, may ascend even in vapor and appear as a cloud, yet retain unchanging the nature and properties of its essence, so the Russian revolt takes all protean shapes in the process of its expression. Constrained by circumstance to manifest itself as passive discontent, as religious protest, as philosophical dogma, as ethnological sentiment, as negation in criticism, as nihilism in morals, as socialism, as incitement to revolution, or as violence and terrorism, the revolt never varies in its inner being, never changes in its essence, but remains the immutable antithesis of absolutism; in this aspect not tainted with the

immorality of force, or soiled with the shedding
of blood, but fair as the cause of human liberty,
and irradiated with the sunlight of awakened
human consciousness in its struggle with the
darker hemisphere of the national life.

What is true of the various parties who champion the revolt is true also of the demands they
make. Their programmes have an illustrative
but no absolute value. Any reforms that re-
move the grievances out of which the revolt
has arisen will at once make the revolt impossible. At the head of these grievances stands
absolute power. We have already seen to what
a degree this principle is opposed to the racial
sentiment, and contrary to the national traditions. The popular institutions protest against
it. Organizations like the *mir* and the *artel* —
the one representing the agricultural and the
other the urban industries of the country —
alone show how tenaciously the people cling to
the old Slav principle of equality in organization,
and free choice of the instruments of rule. It
is thus not the educated classes alone, but the
masses, — peasant and artisan, land-owner and
student, — of whose aspirations, at least, it may
be said, as it was said of the earliest and freest
Russians, "Neminem ferant imperantem." True
enough it is that amongst the peasants the revolt must long remain in its passive stage. The

glamour which popular superstitions throw around the personal elements of Tsarism is not yet fully dissipated by the brighter illumination of knowledge. Yet year by year, partly owing to educational processes, partly owing to propaganda, even the peasants are being won over to the growing battalions of discontent.

How, then, is the struggle likely to end? Will concession bring it to a premature close, or will the revolt swell finally into revolution? Here it becomes necessary to carry the conflict somewhat beyond the limits within which it has hitherto been confined. The struggle is no mere effort to gain old rights of self-government on the one hand, or to resist encroachments upon power on the other. Stated in its broadest aspect the issue is not only one of Tsarism against constitutional liberty, but of a federative union of Russian Slavs against centralized government. The unified empire was as repugnant to the Russians as absolutism itself. Left to their own free choice they invariably tended to the principle of federalism. Long before the coming of the Varegs, the union between the Russian *volosts* was of a purely federal character. The federal instincts of the people were also shown in the division of the country into appanages. Federalization was, in fact, the inevitable corollary of the

Russian repugnance to sovereignty; to retain power in their own hands the people found it necessary to keep the land divided into a number of small principalities. And that this was no accidental arrangement, but a deliberate policy, is shown by the determination with which they resisted every attempt to unify the divided territories. It was only when all opposition had been broken by force of arms that we at last see Russia centralized, and absolute power building itself a home over the ruins of that federalism which had so effectively sheltered the liberties of the people.

This predilection for federal institutions has tinged the revolt from its inception. Slavophils, Panslavists, and Nihilistic parties have all had schemes in view for securing a federative union of the races composing the Russian empire. In this way the revolt may be said to aim not only at securing constitutional freedom for 36,000,000 Great Russians, but at providing political reforms for the Poles, the Little Russians, the White Russians, Finns, Lithuanians, etc. The Russian revolutionary movement of 1860 drew not a little of its virulence from a federalistic understanding with Polish conspirators of the time. Both Herzen and Bakunin prepared schemes of national federation. Kostomarov, the historian, Shevchenko, the famous poet, and Kulish, the ethnographer, jointly founded the Cyrillo-Methodius Union, the aim of which was the national re-birth of Little Russia, and a federation of all the Russian Slavs. Overtures have from time to time been made to the Cossacks, the Jews, the Esths, the Letts, and even to the Germans of the Baltic provinces,[1] on the basis of a federative alliance against absolutism. The very organization of the revolt itself has been throughout mainly of a federalistic character. The conspirators have never jointly chosen a dictator to direct their movements, nor have they tolerated absolutism in any form. Decentralization has been the strength of terrorism; sporadic activity the main source of its success. To name a leader of the revolt would be difficult, simply because the revolt never had any leader. But in another sense all who champion it are leaders, hence its formidableness.

The issue of the revolt is thus not only an issue of federalism against centralized government: upon the result of the struggle depends the future of Russian imperialism itself. The first act of a popular government would be to replace the existing cohesion of force by a free grouping of at least the Slav elements of the

[1] See *Der Baltische Federalist*, published at Geneva, also the address *An meine baltische Landsleute.*

population in voluntary federation. It needs
no gift of prophecy to predict what would follow. The result would be a change of immense
international significance. The Russian state
would speedily lose its character as an aggressive power. The champions of the revolt love
their country and their race, but for the empire
they have little historical or political affection.
The country is linked with hallowed and sacred
memories; the empire is associated with an endless succession of degradations and sufferings.
In their country the Russians lived as freemen
and happy ; when the empire came, it brought
absolutism, destroyed the communal liberties,
debased the individual, made millions of slaves.
No reader of Russian history need be reminded
that the growth of Russia the empire did not
really begin until Russia the country had been
forced into receiving a ruler of the Byzantine
type to replace the prince elected in popular
assembly as servant and not master of the
people. The moment autocratic power was
established in Russia, that moment the Russian empire began its movement of expansion. From the beginning to the end of the
sixteenth century, a period which represents
the first hundred years of absolutism and centralization in Russia, the territory of the empire was quadrupled. Since the beginning of

17

the seventeenth century it has increased from three millions to eight millions of square miles, in round numbers. Starting from the nuclei of her national life at Kiev, Novgorod, and Moscow, Russia has extended her borders northward and eastward and southward until she presents to the startled geographer and politician a continuous territory equal in surface to that which the moon turns to the earth.[1] And the expansion has been wrought not by the Russian people themselves, but at the expense of the popular liberties; not owing to the sympathetic acquiescence of international spectators, but by sacrifice of the interests, and by overriding of the resistance, of protesting nationalities.

Viewed in the light of these facts, the issue of the revolt is no longer of a partisan or even of a merely national character; it becomes of immense significance for Europe. It is no less than this: shall this vast empire, drawing from tyranny at home its means of aggression abroad, go on in its present path of expansion for a period and with results to which limits cannot even be suggested? Or shall the Russian people, breaking up into peaceful federations, and drawing from recovered popular rights the means of a prosperous internal development, de-

---

[1] Humboldt.

vote themselves thenceforward to a policy of concession at home and non-interference abroad?
The revolt, it should be remembered, not only
opposes internal tyranny: it is the foe of imperial aggrandizement.   A stationary Russia
under absolutism is an impossibility. Retrogres-
sion means ruin to imperial interests. The natural and normal policy of the empire is thus
one which makes Russia a constant menace to
Europe.   That this menace should arise from
an immoral usurpation of popular rights and
liberties shows the close moral *solidarité* of
nations, the intimate dependence of universal
well-being upon universal justice, the impossibility of confining the results of wrong-doing,
and particularly wrong-doing in the form of
offenses against the freedom of a people, to the
country which suffers from them the first. The
nations all have an interest in the removal of
the popular wrong in Russia, since out of that
wrong springs not only the terrorism of the revolt, threatening an imperial integrity which is
not needed, but the terrorism of the empire,
menacing an international integrity which must
be maintained.   The cause of democracy in
Russia is the cause of Europe.   In a community of constitutional governments absolutism
is the common enemy.

The proofs of all this are cumulative. If

Russia is the vastest, she is also the youngest state in Europe.   A like rapidity of development is unknown in history.   The national literature is scarcely more than a century old. The first Russian poet came four hundred years after the English had Chaucer.   Juvenile as a nation, Russia is youthful as a race.   She stands, as Bishop Strossmeyer expressed it, "on the threshold of the morning."   Her day is in the future, and she grows towards it continually. Such is the rate at which her people increase that in half a century the Russian empire will number a population of close upon 158,000,000.[1] How these 158,000,000 of people shall be wielded is, therefore, of immense importance to Europe. If they are wielded from within, with the good sense and prudence that naturally characterize popular self-government, then the nations may look on with sympathy and approval.   But if they are to be wielded by despotism, some new means of protecting Europe from Russian encroachments will have to be devised.   The expansion of the empire means the spread of absolutism; and in this sense, as illustrating an inevitable tendency that must be promoted by not being held in check, it may be said, with

[1] In the absence of wars or exceptional maladies.   The yearly increase of population is, in Russia, 781,000; in Germany, 564,094; in Great Britain, 276,623; France, 96,647. (Russian Official Board of Statistics.)

truth, that if the will of Peter did not exist, Europe would be under the necessity of inventing it.

The revolt in its widest phase I have defined as a tacit alliance of interest between the Russian people and the nations of Europe against a principle and method of government hostile to the common weal. It is the protest of eighty millions of people against their continued employment as a barrier in the path of peaceful human progress and national development. It is the protest of Europe against the utilization of enormous forces of racial growth and reproduction for the organized furtherance of personal ambitions and dynastic wealth. Yet the narrower and more immediate issue is that of a struggle which is purely domestic. The early dissolution of absolutism by force is a contingency the least probable of all. The devoted and ignorant loyalty of the peasant will remain the safeguard of the empire against revolution for many decades yet to come. Terrorism may abolish the individual, but it leaves the principle intact. The most dangerous form of conspiracy known in Russian history, that is to say, military conspiracy, has only succeeded in compassing dynastic changes. Yet autocracy in Russia is none the less doomed. The forces that undermine it are cumulative and relentless. Not terrorism, or nihilism, or socialism, is it that feeds those forces, but civilization, national enlightenment, individual awakening. Hence the true policy of autocracy is to spread its dissolution — after the manner of certain financial operations — over a number of years. It will thus be possible, on the one hand, to avoid a rude shock to imperial *amour propre,* and on the other to afford the due preparation for a comprehensive scheme of constitutional government. But the demand for an immediate and substantial concession is none the less urgent. It might take the form of a temporary convention of popular representatives, chosen in the various governments, or of an admission of delegates of the people to co-deliberation with the members of the Imperial Council (Gosudarstvenny Sovyet), after a scheme said to have been devised by the late Tsar. The method of the change is really not of importance. The vital matter is that the reform shall at once concede and practically apply the principle of popular self-government, granting at the same time the fullest rights of free speech and public assembly. To further procrastinate is simply to purchase a merely temporary immunity from the inevitable, at immense personal and political risk.

Let the Tsar and his advisers beware. The

spectacle of this frightfully unequal struggle — unequal alike in its justifications and in the physical forces which it arrays against each other — is not lost upon Europe, or even upon America. A system that maintains itself by the infliction of human suffering and the negation of human rights cannot long expect to receive from governments the tolerance which is denied to it by peoples. Already nations are beginning to recognize that the standing menace in the east of Europe is not the Russian race, but Russian absolutism; already a greater danger is growing up to the " Emperor of all the Russias " than the danger of constitutional reform. And yet it would be sad if the issues were always to be confined within political limits. Hence it is well that one can look forward to the time when a new conception of international rights and obligations shall take the place of the old; when serried lines of glistening bayonets and smoking cannon will no longer be needed to relieve the struggle for liberty from the reproach of crime; when tyranny shall be an offense against the community of nations, as it is now an offense against the community of individuals, and when countries that have won their own liberty and gone through the bitter day shall gladly repay their glorious gains in noble blows struck for universal freedom.

INDEX.

ABSORPTION, 11.
Acclimatization, 11.
Administrative procedure, 242, 243.
Agriculturists, wandering of, 20; attached to glebe, 21.
Aksakov, 175, 176.
Alexander I., 156, 163, 164, 165.
Alexander II., 155.
Alexander III., 210.
"Annals of the Fatherland," the, 234.
Apolism, results of, 51.
Art, 67, 68.
Assassination; attempt at, by Karakasov, 196; stabbing of Mesentsev, 206; Soloviev's attempt, 207; Alexander II. killed, 209; Sudeikin assassinated, 210.
Astrakhan, commerce of, 40.
Atavism, in eating, 31; in religion, 140.
Authority, protest and revolt against, 131, 139, 140, 160, 161.
Autocracy, 99; doomed, 261; true policy of, 262.
Avakum, 137, 138.

Baku, 39.
Bakunin, 176, 200.
Banishment, without trial, 242.
Beds, 49.
Berdichev, 38.
Bestyuzhev, 167, 171.
Bielinsky, 156, 195, 209.
Black Sea, 39.
Blanc, Louis, 156.
Breakfast, 30.
Büchner, 156.
Buckle, 156.
Byron, 156.
Byzantinism, 93, 95, 96, 98, 177, 186.
Byzantium, 55.

Catherine, 160-162.
Catholic Church, civilization of, 108.
Caucasus, 7.

Censure, 162, 233-235.
Central Asia, 15, 16.
Centralization, opposed by the revolt, 254.
Chaikovtsy Society, 221, 222, 226.
Cheremiss, 10.
Chernishevsky, 156, 157, 195, 197; life of, sketched, 212; banishment, 213; influence, 215; interview with, 215.
Children, beating of, 102.
Chin, evils of, 235, 236.
Christianity, defects of Byzantine, 107, 108.
Chuds, 136.
Cities, lack of, 35; at first of wood, 36; etymology of, 36; eleven largest, 38; contrasted with cities of Western Europe, 54; mere taxable units, 55; deprived of burgher element, 56.
Citizenship, inactivity of, 236.
Civilization, 8; influenced by Mongol invasion, 12; lateness of, 64; early Russian, 176.
Class, distinctions of, 104.
Climate, political effects of, 64, 65.
Colonization, effects of, 127-129; in Russia, 129.
Commune, character of, 87; age of, 90.
Conspiracy, beginnings of, 166; the Petrashevsky, 195; of Nechayev, 199; at Chigirin, 204.
Constantinople, 21.
Contemporary, the, 195, 197, 214, 217.
Cossacks, recruited by fugitive serfs, 21; republic of, destroyed, 161.
Counting frame, 17.
Counting, lack of proficiency in, 17.
Country, vastness of, 23.
Cruelty, of legislation, 102.
Cunning, origin of, 105.

Darwin, 156.

Dazh-bog, the sun-god, 83.
Democracy, Russian, 259.
Derzhaviu, 155.
Despotism, of father, 102 ; of law, 102, 103 ; paralyzed by Peter, 153.
Dissent, motive force of, 142.
Dissenters, 134, 152.
Dobrolyubov, 157, 221.
Domicile, easy change of, 33.
Domiciliary period, beginning of, 42, 43.
Domostroï, the, 31, 32, 95, 96, 102, 118, 120, 147, 157, 159.
Dostoyevsky, 184, 187.
Dram shop, influence of, 239.
Drenteln, 207.
Durachok, Ivanushka, 105.

Education, regulation of, 163, 164.
Emancipation, results of, 240.
Empire, significance of ; national instincts hostile to, 257 ; a creation of autocracy, 257 ; growth of, 258.
Encyclopædists, 165.
Enlightenment, influences of, 146, 147, etc. ; enemy of autocracy, 153 ; welcome of, 154.
Enslavement, of the servant, 101 ; of the peasant, 101 ; of the wife, 110.
Epic songs, 83 ; story of Ilya, 84, 85.
Escapades, 211.
Europe: its relation to the revolt, 253, 254, etc.; revolt and, 261 ; how menaced, 258.
Executive Committee, 208, 209, 237.
Exile, 7 ; number sent into, 210 ; lot of in Siberia, 249, 250.
Explosions : at Winter Palace, 208 ; at Moscow, 208.

Fairs, 22.
Family, becomes an autocracy, 102 ; Europeanized, 107.
Federation, 255-257.
Festivals, 189.
Finns, 10.
Fish, 30.
Food, eaten in memory of dead, 13.
Foreigners, 38.
Foreign tastes, how formed, 74.
Forests, 6 ; as factors of polytheism, 62, 63.
Fourier, 156, 194.
Freemasonry, 166.
Funerals, 13.

Germans, 38.
Godunov, Boris, 21.
Goethe, 156, 181.

Gogol, 37, 48, 155, 156, 173, 184, 187, 227, 236.
Government, character of early Slav, 91.
Great Russian language, 25 ; compared with Turkish tongues, 26 ; with European speech, 27 ; characteristics, 28.
Great Russians, 8, 9, 17.
Greek Church, protest against, 130 ; book controversy, 131, 134 ; collation of texts, 132, 133 ; triumph of the reformers, 133 ; outbreak against, 135 ; union of, with state, 238, 239 ; re-birth of, needed, 240.
Griboyedov, 7, 155, 156.
Grinevsky, life of, 229.
Gurko, 207.

Habits, transmission of, 10, 11 ; Asiatic, 13 ; eating, 29 ; drinking, 30.
Haxthausen, 159.
Hegel, 156, 173.
Helfmann, Hesse, 210.
Herberstein, cited, 15, 16, 29, 106.
Herzen, 176, 177, 187.
History, 8.
Hospitality, 81-83.
House, lack of pride in, 50 ; doors of, ignored by servants, 50 ; domicile of peasant, 51.

Imprisoned, number of, 210.
Individual, freedom of, 86 ; ignored by the Greek Church, 97 ; debasement of, 104.
Individualism, reaction by, 194.
Individuality, quickening of, 130 ; a motive force, 142.
Insurrection, along the Volga, 136 ; of Pugachev, 139, 160 ; of December, 167 ; Polish, 197.
Intermingling, 10, 12.

Jews, 38.
Judges, behavior of, 243, 244.
Judicial reform, 241.

Kalmucks, 32.
Kantimir, 155.
Kapustin, 182.
Karamzin, cited, 42, 86, 88, 102, 155.
Kazan, 39, 40.
Kibalshchich, life of, 228.
Kiev, a place of pilgrimage, 22 ; population, 38.
Killed, number of, 210, 211.
Kinglake, 17.
Kishinev, 38.
Koltsov, 155.

Kostomarov, 118.
Krim, 171; war in, 195.
Krylov, 155.
Kvass, 14, 120.

Landscape, 5, 6; no real pictur-esqueness in, 69.
Language, evidence of, 24; lacks dialects, 25.
Legislature, 89; humanitarian character of, 91; change to cruelty, 102.
Lermontov, 7, 187.
Liberties, eclipse of, 101.
Linguists, Russians as, 17-19.
Literati, 155.
Literature, 7, 155, 156.
Little Russia, serfage established in, 161.
Love, 122.
Lying, origin of, 105.

Malthus, 214.
Manners at table, 31, 32; domestic, 31; of early Russians, 80.
Marriage, 124, 125.
Materialism, 158.
Maximus, 132.
Meals, 29.
Melikov, Loris, 242.
Migrant habits, 20, 23, 52, 56.
Migration, 9, 11, 21, 22; its effect upon Russian development and institutions, 33; of cities, 48.
Mill, John Stuart, 157, 215.
Moleschott, 156.
Mongolism, influence of, 107.
Mongols, 12, 20, 99, 100.
Monomakh, Vladimir, 19.
Monotony, of landscape, 6.
Montesquieu, 156.
Mordva, 10.
Moscow, Herberstein at, 15; population, 38; a genuine Russian city, 40; proverbs about, 40, 41; religious, literary, and industrial significance, 41; an artificial creation, 42; view of, 71; character of dwellers in, 106; insurrection in, 160.
Mountains, lack of, 7.
Municipal government, 53.
Muraviev, 166, 167.
Murder, punished by penalty of death, 103.
Mysticism, 179-185; a part of the revolt, 182.

Nechayev, 199.
Nekrassov, 74, 187, 188.

Nestor, 80, 81.
Nevsky Prospect, the, 48, 206, 210, 236.
Newspapers, suppression of, 233, 234.
Nicholas, 167-169, 171, 193,195.
Nihilism, 193, 194.
Nikolaiev, 39.
Nikon, 132, 134, 151, 194.
Nomad languages, 26.
Novgorod, 48, 88, 112.
Novikov, 161, 176.

Odessa, 38, 39, 225, 226.
Old Believers, excommunicated, 133; at Solovetsky, 135, 151.
Owen, 194.

Panslavism, 177.
Paris, Russian travelers at, 165.
Passport system, harassment of, 250, 251.
Patronymics, 29.
Peasants, 73, 83, 106, 165.
Pechenegs, 10.
People, personification of, 84; government by, 87, 88.
Peróvskaya, Sophie, 202, 203; sketch of, 220, etc.; letter of to mother, 223; execution of 209.
Pessimism, 185-192.
Pestel, 166, 167, 170.
Peter, predilection of, for small apartments, 49; reforms of, 148; significance, character, and work of, 149-151.
Petersburg, 48, 152-154, 175, 190-192, 229, 235, 237, 238.
Petroleum trade, 39.
Pissarev, 156.
Plain, illusions of, 5.
Poland, influence of, 145, 146.
Police, brutality of, 244, 246-250.
Polish language, 25; habits, 32; cities, 37, 38.
Polyans, 81.
Polygamy, 111.
Possoshkov, Ivan, 82.
Poverty, 238.
Priesthood, debasement of, 239.
Princes, rule of, 88, 89.
Prisons: Peter and Paul, 206, 247, 248; Novobelgorod, 247; Kharkov, 248; Kara, 250; food strikes in, 206.
Profession, lack of pride in, 51.
Prosecutions, number of, 210, 211.
Protest, 109.
Prudhon, 156, 194.
Pskov, 48, 88.
Pugachev, 139, 160.

Punishment, of sorcerer, 103; of debtor, 104; corporal, 103.
Pushkin, 7, 70, 184, 187.

Rásin, Stenka, 136.
Realism, 52, 158.
Reform, urgency of, 262.
Religion : ideas of future life, 60; sun worship, 61, 62; intercourse with the dead, 78-80; consolations of paganism, 80; Christianity and its influences, 94; Greek Church, 94, 95; monasticism, 96; political aspects, 97; monotheism, 98; raskol, 109, 142, 181, 183, 239; heresy, 109; protest, 126; communism in, 141; weakness, 239.
Revolt, energy of, 137; progress of, 138; takes form of conspiracy, 161; recognized by authorities, 169; vitality of, 172; federative character of, 177, 178; enters the dynamic period, 193; new policy, 199, 200; propaganda, 200; socialistic phase, 200; pilgrimage to the people, 201; terrorism, 204, 205, etc.; conditions favoring revolt, 237; how it is intensified, 242; true nature of the revolt, 252, etc.; how will it end, 254, significance of, for Europe, 261; federalistic character of, 256; hostile to empire, 259.
Rights, personal, 86.
Rousseau, 156.
Russia, a country apart, 8; country of plains, 9; early territory, 10; Tatar period of, 12, 13; climactic life of, 57; united, 101; Europeanized, 148, 152, 153; sadness of, 187; music, 191; youth of, 260; future population, 260.
Russians, mental powers and characteristics of, 17, 66-68; lingual capacity, 17-19; receptivity, 17; migrant character, 33; lack sentiment of place, 52; political humiliation, 54; individuality, 59; intellect, 65; sadness, 188-190; versatility, 188.
Ryliev, 167, 171.
Ryssakov, 209.

Saltykov, Prince, 234.
Samara, 39.
Samovar, manufacture, 39.
Saratov, population of, 39.
Sassulich, Vyera, shoots Trepov, 205.
Schelling, 156.

Schiller, 156.
Schuyler, cited, 15, 16.
Sects, 21, 139-141.
Serf, enslavement of, 101; emancipation of, 157, 196, 240.
Servility, appearance of, 104, 105.
Shevchenko, 255.
Siberia, 20, 210, 218, 242, 249.
Siesta, 31.
Simon, St., 159, 194.
Slav race, 9; colonies, 12; teeth, vision, physical powers, 16; development, 17; migration, 20; enterprise, 39; residences, 49; characteristics, 49; mythology, 60; altruism, 81; intolerance of rulers, 86; family, 86; golden age, 91.
Slavophilism, 172-176, 194.
Slavs, 8, 11, 16, 19, 20; of the Danube, 35; without houses, 35; living in Oppida, 36; modern habitations of, 49; proposed federation of, 177.
Slavyans, 81.
Socialism, 157, 194.
Societies, 166, 167, 195.
Society, characteristics of Russian, 232.
Solovetsky, insurrection at, 135; fall of, 136.
Soloviev, 9, 10.
Spitting, a Slav habit, 32; its origin, 32, 33.
Spring, effects of, 59.
State, the new, 106.
Steppe, 7.
Stryeltsy, rising and extirpation of, 138, 151.
Students, 18, 23, 156, 104, 207, 238.

Tatar influence, 13; names and nouns, 14; customs, 14; domination, 108.
Tatars, 12, 23, 39, 83, 131.
Tax - gatherer, impositions of, 105, 106.
Tea, 30, 31.
Terem, abolition of, 148.
Third Section, 206, 207.
Tolstoï, Leo, 184, 185, 199.
Torture, sanctioned by Russian code, 103; of prisoners, 246.
Town life, 37; populations, 43-45.
Towns, character and growth of, 44; their appearance, 46, 47, 71.
Travel, migratory character of, 23; natural to natives, 23; encouraged by railway freaks, 24.
Tsar, 13.

Tsarism, popular superstitions concerning, 254.
Tsaritsyn, 39, 40.
Tula, 39.
Turanians, 10.
Turgeniev, 15, 155, 184.
Tyranny, fiscal, 56 ; domestic, 115.

Urals, 8.
Urban life, insignificance of, 37, etc.
Uvarov, 169, 170.

Vagabond hunting, 22.
Varega, 87, 88, 90.
Veché, 87, 88, 89, 91, 92, 99, 176.
Vereshchagin, 17.
Viatka, 48, 88.
Village life, beggarliness of, 70.
Vladimir, 82, 108.
Volga, commerce on, 39 ; burlaki and songs, 187 ; propaganda along, 204.
Voronezh, congress at, 208.

Wandering, habit of, 21 ; its modern forms, 22.

West, influence of, 145.
Western ideas, fear of, 164.
Westerns, 174.
Winter, its aspects and appeal to the imagination, 58, 59 ; a despotism, 62 ; enemy of Mongolism, 65.
Women, 72, 73, 74 ; punishment of, 103 ; characteristics, 141 ; devotion of, 112 ; treatment and position, 113, 114, 115, 117 ; relation to husband, 115 ; distrusted by church, 116 ; chastisement of, sanctioned and enjoined, 118 ; seclusion of, 121, 122 ; at Moscow, 123 ; ignorance, 123 ; proverbs regarding, 123, 124 ; influence of in sects, 144 ; emancipation of, 147 ; condition of, in 1843, 159 ; eccentricities of, 159.

Zemlya i Volya, 207, 209.
Zheliabov, 209 ; sketch of, 225, etc. ; executed, 209.
Zhukovsky, 155.

Standard and Popular Library Books

SELECTED FROM THE CATALOGUE OF

HOUGHTON, MIFFLIN AND COMPANY.

JOHN ADAMS and Abigail Adams.
Familiar Letters of, during the Revolution. 12mo, $2.00.

Oscar Fay Adams.
Handbook of English Authors. 16mo, 75 cents.
Handbook of American Authors. 16mo, 75 cents.

Louis Agassiz.
Methods of Study in Natural History. Illus. 16mo, $1.50.
Geological Sketches. Series I. and II., each, 16mo, $1.50.
A Journey in Brazil. Illustrated. 8vo, $5.00.
Life and Letters. Edited by his wife. 2 vols. (*In Press.*)

Thomas Bailey Aldrich.
Story of a Bad Boy. Illustrated. 12mo, $1.50.
Marjorie Daw and Other People. 12mo, $1.50.
Prudence Palfrey. 12mo, $1.50.
The Queen of Sheba. 16mo, $1.50.
The Stillwater Tragedy. 12mo, $1.50.
From Ponkapog to Pesth. 16mo, $1.25.
Poems, Complete. Illustrated. 8vo, $5.00.
Mercedes, and Later Lyrics. Crown 8vo, $1.25.

Rev. A. V. G. Allen.
Continuity of Christian Thought. 12mo, $2.00.

American Commonwealths.
Virginia. By John Esten Cooke.
Oregon. By William Barrows.
Maryland. By Wm. Hand Browne.
Kentucky. By N. S. Shaler.

(In Preparation.)

Michigan. By Hon. T. M. Cooley.
Kansas. By Leverett W. Spring.
Pennsylvania. By Hon. Wayne MacVeagh.
California. By Josiah Royce.
South Carolina. By Hon. W. H. Trescot.
Connecticut. By Alexander Johnston.
Tennessee. By James Phelan.
New York. By Ellis H. Roberts.
Missouri. By Lucien Carr.
        Each volume, 16mo, $1.25.

American Men of Letters.

Washington Irving. By Charles Dudley Warner.
Noah Webster. By Horace E. Scudder.
Henry D. Thoreau. By Frank B. Sanborn.
George Ripley. By O. B. Frothingham.
J. Fenimore Cooper. By Prof. T. R. Lounsbury.
Margaret Fuller Ossoli. By T. W. Higginson.
Ralph Waldo Emerson. By Oliver Wendell Holmes.
Edgar Allan Poe. By George E. Woodberry.
Nathaniel Parker Willis. By H. A. Beers.

(In Preparation.)

Nathaniel Hawthorne. By James Russell Lowell.
Edmund Quincy. By Sydney Howard Gay.
William Cullen Bryant. By John Bigelow.
Bayard Taylor. By J. R. G. Hassard.
William Gilmore Simms. By George W. Cable.
Benjamin Franklin. By John Bach McMaster.
        Each volume, with Portrait, 16mo, $1.25.

American Statesmen.

John Quincy Adams. By John T. Morse, Jr.
Alexander Hamilton. By Henry Cabot Lodge.
John C. Calhoun. By Dr. H. von Holst.
Andrew Jackson. By Prof. W. G. Sumner.
John Randolph. By Henry Adams.
James Monroe. By Pres. D. C. Gilman.
Thomas Jefferson. By John T. Morse, Jr.
Daniel Webster. By Henry Cabot Lodge.

Albert Gallatin. By John Austin Stevens.
James Madison. By Sydney Howard Gay.
John Adams. By John T. Morse, Jr.
John Marshall. By Allan B. Magruder.
Samuel Adams. By J. K. Hosmer.

(*In Preparation.*)
Henry Clay. By Hon. Carl Schurz.
Martin Van Buren. By Hon. Wm. Dorsheimer.
Each volume, 16mo, $1.25.

Mrs. Martha Babcock Amory.
Life of John Singleton Copley. 8vo, $3.00.

Hans Christian Andersen.
Complete Works. 10 vols. 12mo, each $1.50.
New Edition. 10 vols. 12mo, $10.00. (*Sold only in sets.*)

Francis, Lord Bacon.
Works. 15 vols. crown 8vo, $33.75.
Popular Edition. With Portraits. 2 vols. crown 8vo, $5.00.
Promus of Formularies and Elegancies. 8vo, $5.00.
Life and Times of Bacon. 2 vols. crown 8vo, $5.00.

Maturin M. Ballou.
Due West. Crown 8vo, $1.50.

E. D. R. Bianciardi.
At Home in Italy. 16mo, $1.25.

William Henry Bishop.
The House of a Merchant Prince. A Novel. 12mo, $1.50.
Detmold. A Novel. 18mo, $1.25.
Choy Susan and other Stories. 16mo, $1.25.

Björnstjerne Björnson.
Norwegian Novels. 7 vols. 16mo, each $1.00.
New Edition. 3 vols. 16mo, the set, $4.50.

Anne C. Lynch Botta.
Handbook of Universal Literature. 12mo, $2.00.

British Poets.
Riverside Edition. Crown 8vo, each $1.75 ; the set, 68 vols.,
$100.00.

John Brown, M. D.

Spare Hours. 3 vols. 16mo, each $1.50.

Robert Browning.

Poems and Dramas, etc. 15 vols. 16mo, $22.00.
Complete Works. *New Edition.* 7 vols. crown 8vo, $12.00.
Ferishtah's Fancies. 16mo, $1.00 ; crown 8vo, $1.00.

William Cullen Bryant.

Translation of Homer. The Iliad. 1 vol. crown 8vo, $3.00.
2 vols. royal 8vo, $9.00 ; crown 8vo, $4.50.
The Odyssey. 1 vol. crown 8vo, $3.00. 2 vols. royal 8vo,
$9.00 ; crown 8vo, $4.50.

John Burroughs.

Works. 6 vols. 16mo, each $1.50.

Thomas Carlyle.

Essays. With Portrait and Index. 4 vols. 12mo, $7.50.
Popular Edition. 2 vols. 12mo, $3.50.

Alice and Phœbe Cary.

Poems. *Household Edition.* 12mo, $2.00.
Library Edition. Including Memorial by Mary Clemmer.
Portraits and 24 illustrations. 8vo, $4.00.

Lydia Maria Child.

Looking toward Sunset. 12mo, $2.50.
Letters. With Biography by Whittier. 16mo, $1.50.

James Freeman Clarke.

Ten Great Religions. Parts I. and II., 8vo, each $3.00.
Common Sense in Religion. 12mo, $2.00.
Memorial and Biographical Sketches. 12mo, $2.00.

John Esten Cooke.

My Lady Pokahontas. 16mo, $1.25.

James Fenimore Cooper.

Works. New *Household Edition.* Illustrated. 32 vols.
16mo, each $1.00 ; the set, $32.00.
Globe Edition. Illustrated. 16 vols. 16mo, $20.00.

Charles Egbert Craddock.
In the Tennessee Mountains. 16mo, $1.25.
The Prophet of the Great Smoky Mountains. (*In Press.*)
Down the Ravine. Illustrated. 16mo, $1.00.

F. Marion Crawford.
To Leeward. 16mo, $1.25.
A Roman Singer. 16mo, $1.25.
An American Politician. 16mo, $1.25.

M. Çreighton.
The Papacy during the Reformation. 2 vols. 8vo, $10.00.

Richard H. Dana.
To Cuba and Back. 16mo, $1.25.
Two Years before the Mast. 12mo, $1.50.

Thomas De Quincey.
Works. 12 vols. 12mo, each $1.50; the set, $18.00.

Madame De Staël.
Germany. 12mo, $2.50.

Charles Dickens.
Works. *Illustrated Library Edition.* With Dickens Dictionary. 30 vols. 12mo, each $1.50; the set, $45.00.
Globe Edition. 15 vols. 16mo, each $1.25; the set, $18.75.

J. Lewis Diman.
The Theistic Argument, etc. Crown 8vo, $2.00.
Orations and Essays. Crown 8vo, $2.50.

F. S. Drake.
Dictionary of American Biography. 8vo, half calf or half morocco, $8.50.

Elizabethan Dramatists.
Vols. 1–3. Marlowe's Works.
Vols. 4–11. Middleton's Works.
Each vol. $3.00; *Large-Paper Edition*, each vol. $4.00.

George Eliot.
The Spanish Gypsy. A Poem. 16mo, $1.00.

Ralph Waldo Emerson.
Works. *Riverside Ed.* 11 vols. each $1.75 ; the set, $19.25.
"*Little Classic*" Edition. 11 vols. 18mo, each, $1.50.
Parnassus. *Household Edition.* 12mo, $2.00.
Library Edition. 8vo, $4.00.
Poems. *Household Edition.* Portrait. 12mo, $2.00.

F. de S. de la Motte Fénelon.
Adventures of Telemachus. 12mo, $2.25.

James T. Fields.
Yesterdays with Authors. 12mo, $2.00 ; 8vo, $3.00.
Underbrush. 18mo, $1.25.
Ballads and other Verses. 16mo, $1.00.
The Family Library of British Poetry. Royal 8vo, $5.00.
Memoirs and Correspondence. 8vo, $2.00.

John Fiske.
Myths and Mythmakers. 12mo, $2.00.
Outlines of Cosmic Philosophy. 2 vols. 8vo, $6.00.
The Unseen World, and other Essays. 12mo, $2.00.
Excursions of an Evolutionist. 12mo, $2.00.
The Destiny of Man. 16mo, $1.00.

Dorsey Gardner.
Quatre Bras, Ligny, and Waterloo. 8vo, $5.00.

Gentleman's Magazine Library.
14 vols. 8vo, each, $2.50. Roxburgh, $3.50. *Large Paper Edition*, $6.00. I. Manners and Customs. II. Dialect, Proverbs, and Word-Lore. III. Popular Superstitions and Traditions. IV. Archæology — Geological and Historic. (*Last two styles sold only in sets.*)

John F. Genung.
Tennyson's In Memoriam. A Study. Crown 8vo, $1.25.

Johann Wolfgang von Goethe.
Faust. Part First. Translated by C. T. Brooks. 16mo, $1.25.

Faust. Translated by Bayard Taylor. 1 vol. crown 8vo, $3.00. 2 vols. royal 8vo, $9.00 ; 12mo, $4.50.

Correspondence with a Child. 12mo, $1.50.

Wilhelm Meister. Translated by Carlyle. 2 vols. 12mo, $3.00.

Anna Davis Hallowell.

James and Lucretia Mott. Crown 8vo, $2.00.

Arthur Sherburne Hardy.

But Yet a Woman. *Twentieth Thousand.* 16mo, $1.25.

Bret Harte.

Works. *New Edition.* 5 vols. Crown 8vo, each $2.00.

In the Carquinez Woods. 18mo, $1.00.

Flip, and Found at Blazing Star. 18mo, $1.00.

On the Frontier. 18mo, $1.00.

Poems. *Household Edition.* 12mo, $2.00. *Red-Line Edition.* Small 4to, $2.50. *Diamond Edition*, $1.00.

Nathaniel Hawthorne.

Works. *"Little Classic"* Edition. Illustrated. 25 vols. 18mo, each $1.00 ; the set $25.00.

New Riverside Edition. Introductions by G. P. Lathrop. 11 Etchings and Portrait. 12 vols. crown 8vo, each $2.00.

Wayside Edition. With Introductions, Etchings, etc. 24 vols. 12mo, $36.00. (*Sold only in sets.*)

John Hay.

Pike County Ballads. 12mo, $1.50.

Castilian Days. 16mo, $2.00.

Rev. S. E. Herrick.

Some Heretics of Yesterday. Crown 8vo, $1.50.

George S. Hillard.

Six Months in Italy. 12mo, $2.00.

Oliver Wendell Holmes.

Poems. *Household Edition.* 12mo, $2.00.

Illustrated Library Edition. 8vo, $4.00.

Handy-Volume Edition. 2 vols. 18mo, $2.50.

The Autocrat of the Breakfast-Table. Crown 8vo, $2.00.

Handy-Volume Edition. 18mo, $1.25.

The Professor at the Breakfast-Table.   Crown 8vo, $2.00.
The Poet at the Breakfast-Table.   Crown 8vo, $2.00.
Elsie Venner.   Crown 8vo, $2.00.
The Guardian Angel.   Crown 8vo, $2.00.
Medical Essays.   Crown 8vo, $2.00.
Pages from an old Volume of Life.   Crown 8vo, $2.00.
John Lothrop Motley.   A Memoir.   16mo, $1.50.
Illustrated Poems.   8vo, $5.00.

Blanche Willis Howard.

One Summer.   18mo, $1.25.   Illustrated.   Square 12mo, $2.50.
One Year Abroad.   18mo, $1.25.

William D. Howells.

Venetian Life.   12mo, $1.50.
Italian Journeys.   12mo, $1.50.
Their Wedding Journey.   Illus.   12mo, $1.50 ; 18mo, $1.25.
Suburban Sketches.   Illustrated.   12mo, $1.50.
A Chance Acquaintance.   Illus.   12mo, $1.50 ; 18mo, $1.25.
A Foregone Conclusion.   12mo, $1.50.
The Lady of the Aroostook.   12mo, $1.50.
The Undiscovered Country.   12mo, $1.50.

Thomas Hughes.

Tom Brown's School-Days at Rugby.   16mo, $1.00.
Tom Brown at Oxford.   16mo, $1.25.
The Manliness of Christ.   16mo, $1.00 ; paper, 25 cents.

William Morris Hunt.

Talks on Art.   Series I. and II.   8vo, each $1.00.

Thomas Hutchinson.

Diary and Letters.   8vo, $5.00.

Henry James, Jr.

A Passionate Pilgrim and other Tales.   12mo, $2.00.
Transatlantic Sketches.   12mo, $2.00.
Roderick Hudson.   12mo, $2.00.
The American.   12mo, $2.00.
Watch and Ward.   18mo, $1.25.
The Europeans.   12mo, $1.50.

Confidence. 12mo, $1.50.
The Portrait of a Lady. 12mo, $2.00.

Mrs. Anna Jameson.
Writings upon Art Subjects. 10 vols. 18mo, each $1.50.

Sarah Orne Jewett.
Deephaven. 18mo, $1.25.
Old Friends and New. 18mo, $1.25.
Country By-Ways. 18mo, $1.25.
Play-Days. Stories for Children. Square 16mo, $1.50.
The Mate of the Daylight. 18mo, $1.25.
A Country Doctor. 16mo, $1.25.
A Marsh Island. 16mo, $1.25.

Rossiter Johnson.
Little Classics. Eighteen handy volumes containing the choicest Stories, Sketches, and short Poems in English Literature. Each in one vol. 18mo, $1.00 ; the set, $18.00. 9 vols. square 16mo, $13.50. (*Sold only in sets.*)

Samuel Johnson.
Oriental Religions: India, 8vo, $5.00. China, 8vo, $5.00. Persia, 8vo, $5.00.
Lectures, Essays, and Sermons. Crown 8vo, $1.75.

Charles C. Jones, Jr.
History of Georgia. 2 vols. 8vo, $10.00.

Omar Khayyám.
Rubáiyát. *Red-Line Edition.* Square 16mo, $1.00.
The Same. With 56 illustrations by Vedder. Folio, $25.00.

T. Starr King.
Christianity and Humanity. With Portrait. 16mo, $2.00.
Substance and Show. 16mo, $2.00.

Lucy Larcom.
Poems. 16mo, $1.25.   An Idyl of Work. 16mo, $1.25.
Wild Roses of Cape Ann and other Poems. 16mo, $1.25.
Breathings of the Better Life. 16mo, $1.25.
Poems. New *Household Edition.* 12mo, $2.00.

George Parsons Lathrop.

A Study of Hawthorne.   18mo, $1.25.
An Echo of Passion.   16mo, $1.25.

Henry C. Lea.

Sacerdotal Celibacy.   8vo, $4.50.

Charles G. Leland.

The Gypsies.   Crown 8vo, $2.00.
Algonquin Legends of New England.   Crown 8vo, $2.00.

George Henry Lewes.

The Story of Goethe's Life.   Portrait.   12mo, $1.50.
Problems of Life and Mind.   5 vols. 8vo, $14.00.

J. G. Lockhart.

Life of Sir W. Scott.   3 vols. 12mo, $4.50.

Henry Cabot Lodge.

Studies in History.   Crown 8vo, $1.50.

Henry Wadsworth Longfellow.

Poetical Works.   *Cambridge Edition.*   4 vols. 12mo, $9.00.
Poems.   *Octavo Edition.*   Portrait and 300 illustrations, $8.00.
Household Edition.   Portrait.   12mo, $2.00.
Red-Line Edition.   Portrait and 12 illus.   Small 4to, $2.50.
Diamond Edition. $1.00.
Library Edition.   Portrait and 32 illustrations.   8vo, $4.00.
Christus. *Household Edition,* $2.00 ; *Diamond Edition,* $1.00.
Prose Works.   *Cambridge Edition.*   2 vols. 12mo, $4.50.
Hyperion.   16mo, $1.50.   Kavanagh.   16mo, $1.50.
Outre-Mer.   16mo, $1.50.   In the Harbor.   16mo, $1.00.
Michael Angelo : a Drama.   Illustrated.   Folio, $7.50.
Twenty Poems.   Illustrated.   Small 4to, $4.00.
Translation of the Divina Commedia of Dante.   1 vol.
   cr. 8vo, $3.00.   3 vols. royal 8vo, $13.50 ; cr. 8vo, $6.00.
Poets and Poetry of Europe.   Royal 8vo, $5.00.
Poems of Places.   31 vols., each $1.00 ; the set, $25.00.

James Russell Lowell.

Poems. *Red-Line Edition.* Portrait. Illus. Small 4to, $2.50.
Household Edition.   Portrait.   12mo, $2.00.
Library Edition.   Portrait and 32 illustrations.   8vo, $4.00.

Diamond Edition. $1.00.
Fireside Travels. 12mo, $1.50.
Among my Books. Series I. and II. 12mo, each $2.00.
My Study Windows. 12mo, $2.00.

Thomas Babington Macaulay.
Complete Works. 8 vols. 12mo, $10.00.

Harriet Martineau.
Autobiography. Portraits and illus. 2 vols. 12mo, $4.00.
Household Education. 18mo, $1.25.

G. W. Melville.
In the Lena Delta. Maps and Illustrations. 8vo, $2.50.

Owen Meredith.
Poems. *Household Edition.* Illustrated. 12mo, $2.00.
Library Edition. Portrait and 32 illustrations. 8vo, $4.00.
Lucile. *Red-Line Edition.* 8 illustrations. Small 4to, $2.50.
Diamond Edition. 8 illustrations. $1.00.

S. Weir Mitchell.
In War Time. 16mo, $1.25.

J. W. Mollett.
Illustrated Dictionary of Words used in Art and Archæology. Small 4to, $5.00.

Michael de Montaigne.
Complete Works. Portrait. 4 vols. 12mo, $7.50.

William Mountford.
Euthanasy. 12mo, $2.00.

T. Mozley.
Reminiscences of Oriel College, etc. 2 vols. 16mo, $3.00.

Elisha Mulford.
The Nation. 8vo, $2.50.
The Republic of God. 8vo, $2.00.

T. T. Munger.
On the Threshold. 16mo, $1.00.
The Freedom of Faith. 16mo, $1.50.
Lamps and Paths. 16mo, $1.00.

J. A. W. Neander.
History of the Christian Religion and Church, with Index volume, 6 vols. 8vo, $20.00 ; Index alone, $3.00.

Joseph Neilson.
Memories of Rufus Choate. 8vo, $5.00.

Charles Eliot Norton.
Notes of Travel and Study in Italy. 16mo, $1.25.
Translation of Dante's New Life. Royal 8vo, $3.00.

G. H. Palmer.
Translation of Homer's Odyssey. Books 1–12. 8vo, $2.50.

James Parton.
Life of Benjamin Franklin. 2 vols. 8vo, $4.00.
Life of Thomas Jefferson. 8vo, $2.50.
Life of Aaron Burr. 2 vols. 8vo, $5.00.
Life of Andrew Jackson. 3 vols. 8vo, $7.50.
Life of Horace Greeley. 8vo, $2.50.
General Butler in New Orleans. 8vo, $2.50.
Humorous Poetry of the English Language. 8vo, $2.00.
Famous Americans of Recent Times. 8vo, $2.50.
Life of Voltaire. 2 vols. 8vo, $6.00.
The French Parnassus. 12mo, $2.00 ; crown 8vo, $3.50.
Captains of Industry. 16mo, $1.25.

Blaise Pascal.
Thoughts. 12mo, $2.25.   Letters. 12mo, $2.25.

Elizabeth Stuart Phelps.
The Gates Ajar. 16mo, $1.50.
Beyond the Gates. 16mo, $1.25.
Men, Women, and Ghosts. 16mo, $1.50.
Hedged In. 16mo, $1.50.
The Silent Partner. 16mo, $1.50.
The Story of Avis. 16mo, $1.50.
Sealed Orders, and other Stories. 16mo, $1.50.
Friends : A Duet. 16mo, $1.25.
Doctor Zay. 16mo, $1.25.
Songs of the Silent World. 16mo, gilt top, $1.25.

Mrs. S. M. B. Piatt.
An Irish Garland. 16mo, $1.00.

Carl Ploetz.
Epitome of Universal History. 12mo, $3.00.

Adelaide A. Procter.
Poems. *Diamond Ed.* $1.00. *Red-Line Ed.* Sm. 4to, $2.50.

C. F. Richardson.
Primer of American Literature. 18mo, 30 cents.

Riverside Aldine Series.
Each volume, 16mo, $1.00.
1. Marjorie Daw, etc. By T. B. ALDRICH.
2. My Summer in a Garden. By C. D. WARNER.
3. Fireside Travels. By J. R. LOWELL.
4. The Luck of Roaring Camp, etc. By BRET HARTE.
5. Venetian Life. 2 vols. By W. D. HOWELLS.
6. Wake Robin. By JOHN BURROUGHS.

Henry Crabb Robinson.
Diary, Reminiscences, etc. Crown 8vo, $2.50.

Josiah Royce.
Religious Aspect of Philosophy. 12mo, $2.00.

Edgar Saltus.
Balzac. Crown 8vo, $1.25.

John Godfrey Saxe.
Poems. *Red-Line Edition.* Illustrated. Small 4to, $2.50.
Diamond Edition. $1.00. *Household Edition.* 12mo, $2.00.

Sir Walter Scott.
Waverley Novels. *Illustrated Library Edition.* 25 vols.
12mo, each $1.00; the set, $25.00.
Globe Edition. 100 illustrations. 13 vols. 16mo, $16.25.
Tales of a Grandfather. 3 vols. 12mo, $4.50.
Poems. *Red-Line Edition.* Illustrated. Small 4to, $2.50.
Diamond Edition. $1.00.

W. H. Seward.
Works. 5 vols. 8vo, $15.00.
Diplomatic History of the War. 8vo, $3.00.

John Campbell Shairp.

Culture and Religion.   16mo, $1.25.
Poetic Interpretation of Nature.   16mo, $1.25.
Studies in Poetry and Philosophy.   16mo, $1.50.
Aspects of Poetry.   16mo, $1.50.

William Shakespeare.

Works.   Edited by R. G. White.   *Riverside Edition.*   3 vols.
crown 8vo, $7.50 ; The Same.   6 vols. 8vo, $15.00.

A. P. Sinnett.

Esoteric Buddhism.   16mo, $1.25.

Dr. William Smith.

Bible Dictionary.   *American Edition.*   4 vols. 8vo, $20.00.

Edmund Clarence Stedman.

Poems.   *Farringford Edition.*   Portrait.   16mo, $2.00.
Household Edition.   Portrait.   12mo, $2.00.
Victorian Poets.   12mo, $2.00.
Edgar Allan Poe.   An Essay.   Vellum, 18mo, $1.00.

Harriet Beecher Stowe.

Agnes of Sorrento ; The Pearl of Orr's Island ; The Minis-
ter's Wooing ; The May-flower ; Nina Gordon ; Oldtown
Folks ; Sam Lawson's Fireside Stories, etc., illustrated ;
My Wife and I, illustrated ; We and Our Neighbors, il-
lustrated ; Poganuc People, illustrated.   Each volume,
12mo, uniform, $1.50.
A Dog's Mission ; Little Pussy Willow ; Queer Little Peo-
ple.   Each, illustrated, small 4to, $1.25.
Uncle Tom's Cabin.   100 illustrations.   8vo, $3.50.
Popular Edition.   Illustrated.   12mo, $2.00.

Jonathan Swift.

Works.   *Edition de Luxe.*   19 vols. 8vo, the set, $76.00.

Bayard Taylor.

Poetical Works.   *Household Edition.*   12mo, $2.00.
Melodies of Verse.   18mo, vellum, $1.00.
Life and Letters.   2 vols. 8vo, $4.00.

Alfred Tennyson.

Poems. *Household Edition.* Portrait and illus. 12mo, $2.00.
Illustrated Crown Edition. 2 vols. 8vo, $5.00.
Library Edition. Portrait and 60 illustrations. 8vo, $4.00.
Red-Line Edition. Portrait and illus. Small 4to, $2.50.
Diamond Edition. $1.00.

Celia Thaxter.

Among the Isles of Shoals. 18mo, $1.25.
Poems. Small 4to, $1.50.
Drift-Weed. 18mo, $1.50.
Poems for Children. Illustrated. Small 4to, $1.50.

Edith M. Thomas.

A New Year's Masque and other Poems. 16mo, $1.50.

Joseph P. Thompson.

American Comments on European Questions. 8vo, $3.00.

Joseph Thomson.

Through Masai Land. 8vo, $5.00.

Henry D. Thoreau.

Works. 9 vols. 12mo, each $1.50 ; the set, $13.50.

George Ticknor.

History of Spanish Literature. 3 vols. 8vo, $10.00.
Life, Letters, and Journals. Portraits. 2 vols. 12mo, $4.00.

Charles Dudley Warner.

My Summer in a Garden. 16mo, $1.00.
Illustrated Edition. Square 16mo, $1.50.
Saunterings. 18mo, $1.25.
Back-Log Studies. Illustrated. Square 16mo, $1.50.
Baddeck, and that Sort of Thing. 18mo, $1.00.
My Winter on the Nile. Crown 8vo, $2.00.
In the Levant. Crown 8vo, $2.00.
Being a Boy. Illustrated. Square 16mo, $1.50.
In the Wilderness. 18mo, 75 cents.
A Roundabout Journey. 12mo, $1.50.

William F. Warren, LL. D.

Paradise Found. Crown 8vo, $2.00.

William A. Wheeler.

Dictionary of Noted Names of Fiction.   12mo, $2.00.

Edwin P. Whipple.

Essays.   6 vols. crown 8vo, each $1.50.

Richard Grant White.

Every-Day English.   12mo, $2.00.
Words and their Uses.   12mo, $2.00.
England Without and Within.   12mo, $2.00.
The Fate of Mansfield Humphreys.   16mo, $1.25.

Mrs. A. D. T. Whitney.

Stories.   12 vols. each, $1.50.
Mother Goose for Grown Folks.   12mo, $1.50.
Pansies.   Square 16mo, $1.50.
Just How.   16mo, $1.00.

John Greenleaf Whittier.

Poems.   *Household Edition.*   Portrait.   12mo, $2.00.
Cambridge Edition.   Portrait.   3 vols.   12mo, $6.75.
Red-Line Edition.   Portrait.   Illustrated.   Small 4to, $2.50.
Diamond Edition. $1.00.
Library Edition.   Portrait.   32 illustrations.   8vo, $4.00.
Prose Works.   *Cambridge Edition.*   2 vols. 12mo, $4.50.
The Bay of Seven Islands.   Portrait.   16mo, $1.00.
John Woolman's Journal.   Introduction by Whittier. $1.50.
Child Life in Poetry.   Selected by Whittier.   Illustrated.
   12mo, $2.25.   Child Life in Prose.   12mo, $2.25.
Songs of Three Centuries.   Selected by J. G. Whittier.
   Household Edition.   12mo, $2.00.   *Library Edition.*   32
   illustrations.   8vo, $4.00.
Text and Verse.   18mo, 75 cents.

Woodrow Wilson.

Congressional Government.   16mo, $1.25.

J. A. Wilstach.

Translation of Virgil's Works.   2 vols. cr. 8vo, $5.00.

Justin Winsor.

Reader's Handbook of American Revolution.   16mo, $1.25.

www.ingramcontent.com/pod-product-compliance
Lightning Source LLC
Chambersburg PA
CBHW030625030726
47497CB00006B/1645